FREE YOUR TIME:

HOW ASSISTANTS SUPERCHARGE SUCCESSFUL AUTHORS

FREE YOUR TIME
BOOK 1

GRACE SNOKE

Foreword by
MARTHA CARR

SPIDERWEBZ DESIGN, LLC

Book Cover by INKMagine & Create Studios

First edition 2022

Ebook ISBN-13: 979-8-9872190-0-3

Paperback ISBN-13: 979-8-9872190-1-0

❋ Created with Vellum

For Martha Carr and Craig Martelle
Thank you for believing in me.

CONTENTS

WHAT TASKS CAN AN ASSISTANT TAKE ON?

PART ONE
ARC TEAM MANAGEMENT

PART TWO
ADS

PART TEN
SOCIAL MEDIA

PART ONE
MANAGING ACCOUNTS

PART TWO
TOOLS FOR SCHEDULING

PART FIFTEEN
MISCELLANEOUS

QUESTIONS TO ASK YOURSELF

QUESTIONS TO ASK YOUR POTENTIAL ASSISTANT

IMPORTANT THINGS TO REMEMBER

OTHER QUESTIONS

FOREWORD

Grace Snoke is one of the best assistants in the business of indie publishing. Whatever advice she's handing out—take it and run with it—whether you're the assistant or someone looking for one. Your life will be better for it. How do I know?

I've been a professional writer for over thirty years as a journalist, national columnist and now a bestselling author. Last year, in partnership, I made over seven figures and still had a life. Without an assistant that may not have happened. I mean, what's the point of doing well if there's no life to back it up? I'm an eternally curious person so I'm always trying something new. Sky diving, kayaking, gardening an entire yard, cooking lessons, building a magical forest in my front yard for Halloween. You know, the usual.

And, because there's someone like Grace backing me up, I can spend my work hours creating magical worlds with words. Not working overtime on the nitty gritty of newsletters, contests, promotions, remembering deadlines and a thousand other details.

The proof of what I'm saying is in my experience. We have been together for over three and a half years and the income has only risen while the peace and balance have remained, even though the workload has increased.

But is it for you?

If you're thinking of becoming an assistant, you may be asking, do you have the right skillset? What exactly is this author going to expect? This book will be the best shortcut you're ever going to receive that will help shorten the learning curve and increase your appeal to authors.

For the word warriors out there, questions arise like: 'do you really need an assistant? Is it just to make more money? What are the priorities? Can you even afford to pay someone else?'

Those are the questions I'd be asking myself if I'd never had somebody helping me.

The answer to the first question is yes, if you're going to be a professional author who cares about the work as well as the income—an assistant will become more and more necessary.

Oddly, it is the one area of our business that does not get as much coverage as ads, covers or blurbs, but it is just as important. Everything outside of writing could easily eat up all the time for writing without help.

The best question then, is how to spot a good assistant—or become a great one. That's why this book is so timely. Grace is laying it all out there so that others can follow in our footsteps. And now it is your turn. The adventure awaits.

Martha Carr

INTRODUCTION TO P.A./V.A.S

WHAT IS A PERSONAL ASSISTANT/VIRTUAL ASSISTANT AND IS THERE A DIFFERENCE BETWEEN THE TERMS?

A personal assistant is an individual who helps another person with tasks they need to do/have done/keep track of. Often a personal assistant will keep track of upcoming events, order items you need, make sure your calendar is up to date, handle assorted tasks for you, help you at events, etc. They work closely with the person and live in the same city/state in order to interact on an in-person basis. Actors and actresses, CEOs, presidents of companies and other individuals often have one or more personal assistants to help with their day-to-day activities.

A virtual assistant is one who does everything from a remote location. The job tasks can be the same as a personal assistant or vary depending on what the client needs.

For indie authors, or even traditional or hybrid authors, having an assistant or team of assistants will help you build and grow your author business. The more books you have, the longer it takes to handle the admin side of things. What you will find is that your valuable writing time becomes cluttered with tasks that suck time away from writing your next book.

Eventually, in order to keep writing, you need to pay someone for help.

Since an author can have a virtual assistant, a personal assistant, or both, I will be using 'assistant' as an all-inclusive term in this book.

WHY HIRE A P.A./V.A.?

There are many reasons you should hire an assistant to help you with your author business.

While the most important reason is so that you can focus on writing your next book, but there are other reasons as well, such as:

———

1. An assistant means you do not have to do everything yourself.

Being an indie author often means doing many tasks yourself. Those tasks include, but are not limited to:

- writing your books
- self-editing your books
- sending copies of your books to beta readers
- compiling feedback, making changes and sending your books to an editor(s)

And all the other steps involved before hitting publish on your book.

Then there are all the business administration tasks that go into a successful author business:

- Figuring out keywords for ads
- Social media posting
- Newsletter building and distribution
- AMS marketing
- Other marketing
- Blog posts

And so much more...

As your backlist gets bigger, these tasks get longer and more complex. More in-depth planning has to go into everything besides writing and publishing.

Something has to give or you run out of time in your day to write, and as the saying goes, nothing sells your backlist like your next book. But if you do not have time to write your next book, then you will not be selling as many.

———

2. Saves time so you can focus on other things.

There may be some tasks you enjoy doing more than others in addition to writing. Some authors prefer to handle their own social media, or at least some of it. Others like to have their hands on the marketing.

No matter what you prefer to do, having an assistant will allow you to focus on those things, as much or as little as you want.

———

3. An assistant can perform tasks you do not particularly like doing. Or tasks you are not particularly good at or knowledgeable about.

When an indie author starts out, they are often required to become a jack of all trades, handling their own production and marketing. But as you grow your author business, there are some things you will not be good at. And more often than not, there are some tasks you will abhor or find too time consuming to handle yourself.

For example, I know I do not have the time or patience to do my own AMS ads and keyword generation. I know there are experts available who know way more than I do about those, so I would have someone else do that for me.

Other authors prefer to let their assistant schedule newsletter swaps with other authors, handle BookFunnel, and write and send out their newsletters. Those are all things a virtual assistant can do for you.

———

4. But they can also free up your time for other things as well.

Self-care is important. But it is hard to practice self care—no matter how big or small—when you are overwhelmed with everything you have to do before, during and after a book launch.

However, self care is not the only thing an assistant can enable. With a trusted personal or virtual assistant, you could take a vacation and not worry about any problems with your next book launch, or your discount promotion schedule going haywire.

You might be sick and need time to recover—flues and other bugs can be quite nasty and require more recovery time than usual. They require even more time if you are immunocompromised or have other health issues that complicate healing.

You might have emergency surgery (can anyone say appendectomy?) or planned surgery and need additional help to get things done.

The list goes on and on. No matter the reason you need free time for yourself, an assistant is a surefire way to help make that happen.

———

5. And of course, an assistant frees up your time for writing...

You cannot write your next book if you are too busy doing the multitude of things to make your author business run like a well-oiled engine. For most people, the whole reason they became an author was because they loved writing and wanted little to do with outside projects. But being an author means doing more than just writing. Assistants help you spend less time or no time on things that are not writing related.

WHY HIRE MORE THAN ONE ASSISTANT?

There are many reasons and benefits to hiring more than one assistant.

Just like you have a hard time handling all the tasks as your backlist grows, so will your assistants.

If you have more than one pen name, especially if they are in very different genres, you may want more than one for daily tasks and promotions. It makes it easier to keep things organized, while finding someone who is familiar with the genre.

For example, if you write fantasy but also write chick lit, you probably need two different assistants who specialize in those genres because they are quite different for marketing, promotions and social media. Merchandising assistants are flexible across genres, but depending on how extensive your merchandising is, you may want more than one.

———

Specializations

While many assistants will do many tasks, and are good at

some of them, they may not be good at all of them.

For example, I am great at keywords and categories, but I want nothing to do with AMS ads or FB ads. I can assist with keyword farming for ads, but prefer to leave that to someone else. Those who specialize in ads often have the knowhow to pull them quick and easily or already have some keywords already determined for audience and genre.

Some assistants focus on social media scheduling and engagement, including TikTok, Instagram and others. While others focus on merchandizing.

No matter what you are looking for, you are bound to find one or more people able to take on tasks you want to get off your plate.

––––––

You do not risk losing one person who does everything.

Change happens. So does life. If you have only one assistant who handles every aspect of your business that you do not handle, and something happens to them, even temporarily, you will be short staffed.

Whether it is a death in the family, a personal illness, emergency surgery (can you say appendectomy or gallbladder removal?), or a planned vacation, having one person who does everything could be detrimental to your business as well.

If you have one person who does ads and one who handles other tasks, and possibly even a third, then duties can be split up and you, or someone else, can step in when they need a break.

This also allows for transitions to take place easier. If one assistant is leaving to write full time, be a caregiver or something else, it is often easier to find another one who would work with you on what you need filled rather than finding someone who can do everything.

Backup in case tragedy strikes.

As mentioned in the previous reason, as much as we hope tragedy will not happen, it is an eventuality everyone needs to be prepared for. The start of this decade showed many folks just how quick serious illness, injury and death can occur. With the pandemic hitting hard in those two years, many people were called away to help support family or friends with losses.

Even outside of a pandemic, catastrophic illnesses and death can occur for you, the author, or your assistants. As much as we do not want to think about it, it is always possible you could lose that assistant to death as well. Knowing what all your assistant handles, having other people who can step in at a moment's notice (besides yourself), and planning is a great way to handle unfortunate circumstances.

A tragedy may never happen. But in the event it does, at least you have a plan in place to handle any situations that may arise.

You need a team for your author business.

When things overwhelm you, it is time to consider building your team.

Assistants are an integral part of your team. Whether that team is just you and them, or larger, including ad specialists, sales managers and others, an assistant can help you keep everything organized and moving on track.

They can also assist with answering questions for other team members, making sure everyone is on the same page, and insuring things run smoothly while you are away.

WHAT TASKS CAN AN ASSISTANT TAKE ON?

An assistant can take on almost any task you can dream of, if they know how to do it or will learn how to do it. The exception to that being writing story beats, or writing your book for you. You want a ghostwriter for that.

What your assistant takes on first should depend on what they are familiar with and will take on before asking them to consider or learn new tasks. It can take time for an inexperienced assistant to take on tasks and get comfortable enough with them before taking on additional tasks. Be sure to ask them what sort of things they will do. You can create a list of potential tasks they could do by referring to the following chapters of this book.

I am explaining each task because authors who read this are in various states of experience and not everyone has even thought about some tasks, much less how they can be done by an assistant. I expect some authors to be fully knowledgeable about topics and to skim over them, but I hope even those authors find something they may not have thought about.

PART ONE

ARC TEAM MANAGEMENT

Successfully managing an Advanced Reader Review (ARC) Team is important for anyone relying on them to get reviews for their books on release day, or shortly thereafter.

Many things are required to run a successful ARC team. Being organized and capable of tracking and integrating potential changes is just one of many items an assistant can handle. Managing an ARC team can be time-consuming for a new author, but for any author who may want to find someone else to assist in those duties.

Determining what tasks involved in ARC management your assistant can take on is a good point to discuss before they start. Knowing what tasks you want to hold on to, or get rid of, is also a good starting point.

Note: many authors will turn things over to their assistant to handle after giving them guidelines for what they look for in their ARC team.

SCREENING

Adding and removing people from an ARC team is an important part of management. As you gain readers and interest in your books increases, you will have more turnover in your ARC team, but a larger pool of beta readers to draw from. You will want to screen readers to make sure you have people who will read your book on time, and who are proven reviewers.

While leaving reviews on Amazon cannot be a requirement due to Amazon's TOS, you can mandate that to participate in the program, ARC readers to leave reviews on Bookbub, Goodreads and elsewhere, or reviews on their personal blogs or websites.

There are many tools available now to assist with managing ARC teams. Readerlinks, Story Origin and even BookFunnel are great ways to manage your teams. BookSprout and some other sites are other ways to gain ARC readers and get ARC copies to them.

An assistant might use forms within Readerlinks or Story Origin or even set up custom forms with Google Forms or OneDrive forms. These will allow them to gain information they, or you, need to screen the readers and add them to your team if approved.

Be sure to outline what your requirements for an ARC team member are, or let them outline their own if you do not have any.

Also, be sure you outline what requirements you have for a person to stay on the team. Whether it be a certain number of reviews, social media posts, sharing from social media or something else, make sure your assistant knows what those are and that they will talk with members who are not meeting requirements and, when appropriate, are okay with removing them.

They may also decide to re-add these folks at a future time, if real life got to be too much or personal things going on where they could not be active on the team then, but are interested in the future.

Note: you may want your assistant to look at reviews on books other than yours if they have reviews on various sites. It will give them a better overview of the reviews the potential reader gives and whether they would be a good fit.

DISTRIBUTION OF ARCS

ARCs can be distributed many ways. If you have BookFunnel or StoryOrigin, you may want your assistant to set up ARC copies there and use that to distribute it. Or you may give ARC readers a Google Doc where they can only comment with changes. Another option is an ebook file (.ePub or .mobi) they can download through email, Dropbox, Google Drive or other cloud storage platforms.

Your assistant would upload the ARC file wherever you want it to be, make sure who is supposed to receive it does, and remove the file before publication.

And, as they determine who should no longer receive them, remove them from those lists as well.

MANAGE TEAM AND MONITOR PARTICIPATION

Once readers join the ARC team, it is a good idea to make sure they are taking part and not just abusing the system to get free books.

Even though you may hope that all members on your ARC Team will leave reviews, you can not actually require them to leave reviews on specific sites. Some may not review on Amazon because Amazon blocks them for reviewing authors they are friends with. You can strongly encourage them to leave reviews on Goodreads, BookBub, and other sites.

You can also ask your assistant to consider participation which includes liking and sharing posts about upcoming releases on various social media platforms. Or posting about the book themselves. Your assistant can then ask for proof with links to the posts, look at reviews and more.

Then if participation drops off, the assistant can reach out to them and see if they are still interested or not. If there is no response, your assistant can make a decision based on what you want for your ARC teams. For this reason, it is important to give your assistant clear guidelines.

CREATE PRESS KITS FOR ARC/BOOK PROMOTERS

Another thing your assistant can do is create files and zip them together as press kits for your book release.

Things they could put together include:

- Word document with blurb and link to the book
- JPG of the book cover
- Promotional graphics (these could be mockups with praise, reviews, etc.)
- Early reviews
- First chapter if desired
- Author bio, logo, and photo
- Anything else that could promote your release

Once everything is assembled and zipped, they can upload the file to Google Drive, Dropbox, your website, or other locations where your assistant can share it not just with the ARC team, but with people doing newsletter swaps, blog tours, or anyone asking for materials to promote it.

Some kits may remain online indefinitely, especially for future promotions of book ones in a series. Others may need to be pulled down after a time. It is something to discuss and to put in a calendar as a reminder if you decide to pull them down or revoke access.

RUN ARC TEAM CONTESTS

Your assistant can run contests for your ARC team separate from anything related to them leaving reviews. There could be a contest based on who finds the most typos that have made it through editing and proofreading, or for sharing funny quotes from the manuscript in the group (which could be used for promotional graphics), or seeing who can create graphics for sharing.

Whatever you come up with, your assistant can run it for each release, or mix it up. Discuss what you want done and the prizes, and whether or not you are providing them or reimbursing the assistant for purchases.

REWARD ARC TEAM MEMBERS

While you cannot reward your ARC team for leaving reviews on Amazon and other retailers, you can reward them for posting on Goodreads, BookBub, on a blog they own or elsewhere. You can also reward them for sharing releases on their social media, or for their engagement in your Facebook groups or other social media platforms. How often you reward them or what they are rewarded for can be privately known or regularly mentioned to incentivize them.

As with the contests, your assistant can handle tracking whatever metrics are needed for reward tracking, and reward the team members or pass on the information to you for you to reward them yourself.

Whatever you decide, discuss with your assistant how often you want them to be rewarded, what the measurement metrics are, if there are levels to rewards based on participation, who is paying for the prizes initially, and how reimbursement will be handled if your assistant is making the purchases.

PART TWO

ADS

Two-thirds of the authors I consulted with when I started working on this book said that they wanted an assistant that could take over their ads. When I asked what ads, most said Facebook and-or Amazon. A few also wanted Bookbub ads or ads for other platforms.

Ad creation and management is one of the most time-consuming jobs for any assistant to take on, and if they lack experience with it, there is a steep learning curve. If you will train an assistant to do ads the way you want them done and let them learn how to improve upon it as you go, that's great. If you want them to learn as they go, by reading books, then trial and error, that's also great. Just understand the results will not be as good as someone who focuses on ads. If you are looking for someone who specializes in ads, that would be even better. Especially if they will do only ads and not other tasks and which leaves your assistant free to do other stuff.

Keep in mind, you can switch between these at any point. There's no harm in realizing someone is not learning fast enough and you would rather do it yourself, or pay someone who is more experienced than you or an otherwise-assistant to set up and manage your ads.

Even if you want to manage your ads yourself, your assistant can help with related tasks that are time-consuming, including keywords, authors and books to target, target audiences for Facebook and Bookbub and more. This section will go into some of those tasks, but does not cover all tasks as I am not as familiar with advertising and the associated platforms.

DETERMINE WHAT AUTHORS/BOOKS TO TARGET WITH ADS.

A big part of Amazon ads is knowing what other authors and which of their books you want your ads served to when people search for their books. Having your assistant look through Amazon charts and help determine which new books and authors to target will help you decide who you want to target with AMS.

You may still want to audit their lists, especially if they are new to this sort of work. You can start off by letting them know what books are comparable to yours.

For example, if your series is a magical academy, they would search for books in that subgenre, but also look at supernatural academy, paranormal academy, etc. If your book is YA and non-romantic, they would have to weed through the books to make sure they're picking similar YA books with no romance to target. You can give your assistant a list of specific authors to look at or avoid to help with their search.

Finding keywords is a similar task. Often, these two tasks would be done together, but I am separating them because you may wish to review the authors and books they come up with if this is the first time they are doing this for you—especially if they are new to generating keyword lists. It is easier to review things at this stage before they pour too much time into keywords. You do not want to waste time cleaning them up just to find out they used the wrong authors and books.

KEYWORDS

Generating keywords for Amazon is a time-consuming task an assistant can do once trained. Like some of the other tasks an assistant could take on, keywords will take some input from you as an author. They will need to know comparable authors, series, genres and sub-genres to work with to create lists. Those lists also need to be optimized and added to as authors add new series. From that point onward, you can tell them how you want your keyword lists to be built and let them work from there.

I would start with one or two books you want ads done for, especially if the series targets different authors, and see how they do with gathering the data and cleaning it up. Test with ads, then give your assistant feedback on how to improve or to continue with what they're doing.

Determine how often you want them to check for new books and add to or audit keywords, then discuss that with them once you have determined they're a good fit for that task.

TARGET AUDIENCES

Creating target audiences for Facebook ads can be a challenge. You generally cannot target indie authors and must target mainstream authors instead. Targeting mainstream authors can cause higher cost per click.

Your assistant can work on creating target groups that are focused based on your books and audience age, etc. They can also help you with look-a-like audience creation from your mailing list or from people who have already liked your Facebook page or have engaged with the page in the past.

Audiences can change over time too. You may want your assistant to evaluate previous audiences and see if things need to change to keep ads optimized.

Like with the previous items, discussing with your assistant how often you want them to review your ads and their target audience is a good thing. That allows them to mark it in their calendar ahead of time.

FACEBOOK ADS

I will be the first to admit, despite attending multiple Facebook sponsored training events, reading how-to guides, and even experimenting a bit with ads, that Facebook ads are a monster to themselves and they take someone with time, knowledge and patience to set them up, find what works, do A/B testing, and monitor them.

THEN, that has to be done all over again when the ads stop performing or start underperforming. Facebook ads need to be frequently refreshed. It can be a time-consuming process which will suck away time from writing.

Hiring an assistant that is experienced and knowledgeable about Facebook ads and other ad platforms can be a big bonus for driving sales of books and series, running ads to join your newsletter, and generally gaining more visibility on the platform. It can also save you a lot of time because you do not have to do all the administrative work involved with ads. You only have to review them with your marketing assistant from time to time to determine if you want to increase or decrease ad spend, or try something new.

There are many specialized assistants who focus only on Facebook and Amazon Ads (or Facebook and BookBub Ads) and do only ads for their clients. If you are looking to get ads off your plate, looking for a specialized ad person might be a good choice.

Of course, you may have to tell them specific things you've learned from doing your own ads, what your ad spending limits are and so on to help get them started. However, once they know those things, they should be able to run your advertising account with limited check ins. You should let them know how often you want to review how ads are doing and any changes you want or they want to try. You may meet with them more often in the first few months, then space the time out between checks after that.

If you are hiring an experienced Facebook Ads Manager, I would definitely ask them for references and reach out to those references to verify that they did work for them and how they did running ads. You may ask why they parted ways—it may be a case of the author was changing directions or stopped using Facebook Ads and that's why they parted ways, or a personality conflict. If it was something else—for example, they ignored daily or monthly spend limits and repeatedly went way over the limits—you would want to know that before you considering hiring them.

If you cannot find an available specialized assistant, or only want one assistant who will do ads and other tasks for you, you might train an assistant to help with ads. The disadvantage is once you train someone, they can use those skills to help other people in the future. Now, this is not necessarily a bad thing, and I think teaching someone skills that can further their business in the future if they part ways with you is a good thing. But it is something to consider.

You can also just pay them to do certain tasks for you where Facebook ads are concerned that do not require a lot of training, including but not limited to:

- Writing ad copy (this may require training as ad copy is different from other copy writing)

- Creating ad graphics (this may also require training to meet the requirements of the platforms)
- Setting up A/B testing for you to run
- Replying to comments on ads
- Helping to narrow down target audiences and create look-alike audiences
- Determining keywords

You will also have to consider whether they run ads through their Facebook Ad account or if you will add them as an administrator to yours and allow them to use your ad account to run and pay for the ads. The easiest course of action for tracking ad spend and not having to reimburse them for ads each week or month would be to add them to your ad account. This takes a bit of trust that they will not use your account to run ads elsewhere.

No matter if you're hiring a new or an experienced Facebook Ads Manager, you should clearly outline expectations, discuss goals, and what your ROI and CPC/CPM goals are as well as anything you've tried in the past that has or hasn't worked. Communication is important with any assistant, but I find when it comes to ads, it is exponentially more important.

It is important to remember—especially with Facebook—that ad platforms often change how algorithms work. This affects what you have to do to make ads work, so whoever is handling your ads needs to be able to adapt to changes as they happen.

Last, but not least, anyone you bring on to run ads should provide accounting of their ad spends on your behalf. This is true whether or not you are paying for the ads through your account or reimbursing them. There should be detailed spreadsheets of ads being run, CPC rates, etc. In addition, because they may have access to your credit card or PayPal Information, it is only reasonable that they provide regular reports. Perhaps at first on a weekly basis, but after a bit, the reports could come monthly.

AMAZON ADS

Much as with Facebook, I am not an Amazon ads expert and generally refer my clients to other people for this work. That being said, even though I do not manage Amazon ads, there are tasks related to Amazon Ads that I will do, such as keyword curation and maintenance.

Amazon ads are multi-faceted tasks that can be split if necessary. For example, if you want to manage the ads, but do not want to handle the time-consuming part of keyword curation and maintenance, your assistant could do that part of ad management for you.

Or if you have burned out on writing ad copy and want to try some new ads with A/B testing, your assistant could come up with the ad copy to try in combination with new and old keywords. You could even have them handle A/B testing of various ads and report the results back to you.

There are many ways an assistant can help with ads. Whether you are looking to outsource all of your Amazon ad marketing, or just parts of it, finding someone who knows what they are doing or can be trained in how you want your ads to be managed can be a huge timesaver.

As mentioned in the Facebook Ads section above, there are people who specialize in Amazon ads management. They are often in high demand and have waiting lists for clients. Hiring an assistant that is experienced and knowledgeable about Amazon ads and other ad platforms can be a big bonus with driving sales of your books and series. Having someone manage ads in their entirety can save you a lot of time because you do not have to do all the administrative work involved with ads and only have to review them with your marketing assistant from time to time to determine if you want to increase or decrease ad spend, try something new, etc.

If you cannot find an available Amazon ads assistant, or only want one assistant who will do ads and other tasks for you, you might train an assistant to help with ads.

One of the good things about Amazon Ads is that you can add someone as an administrator to your ad account and not give them access to your actual Amazon account or financial information. This allows them to handle everything for the ads while you are being charged for them.

As with Facebook ad managers, if you are hiring an experienced Amazon ads manager, I would ask them for references and reach out to those references to verify that they did work for them and how they did running ads.

It is also important to remember that costs for Amazon ads can change drastically, especially depending on when traditional publishing companies are pushing ad money into the system, when there are new popular books messing with the algorithms and other things. As long as your assistant knows what your max ad spend and cost per click is, they should be able to work with you on when ads should run or paused based on market changes and variations. It might be a good idea to discuss when they see changes and if you want to temporarily increase or decrease your ad spend based on that as well.

BOOKBUB ADS

Bookbub ads are a great way to bring in new readers to your series. They reach targeted readers in your genre, but you are also heavily competing against other authors in the market. That said, Bookbub can be a handy tool in your marketing toolbox.

Bookbub ads, while not as complicated as Facebook and Amazon ads, still require time and testing.

Ideally, an assistant would be able to not only create and test various ads through Bookbub for you but also create necessary ad graphics required to run ads.

As far as I know, with Bookbub ads, you have to give access to your Bookbub account to your assistant for them to handle management of the ads, testing, etc. If you are not comfortable with them having access to your account, you can handle administration tasks while you farm out other tasks for them to do.

If you want to farm out parts of Bookbub ads to an assistant, some tasks they could take on include, but are not limited to:

- Graphic creation (Note: Bookbub ads have very difficult graphic requirements. Any assistant handling them must have excellent graphic design skills)
- Ad copy
- A/B testing
- Authors to target
- Audience targets
- Ad performance analysis (provided you give them the statistics for them to analyze)

Costs for Bookbub ads are variable and expenses can rack up alarmingly quickly in a short period, so make sure you set firm spending goals when running ads on this particular platform.

OTHER ADS

There are other platforms you may be interested in testing out ads on, including but not limited to: Twitter, Pinterest, Google, and TikTok. Each have their advantages and disadvantages and a learning curve to figuring them out.

If you want to branch out into these other platforms, I would strongly suggest finding someone who has had success marketing on those platforms rather than trying to teach someone a new platform you are also learning.

There are several books available about running ads on the various platforms that can provide a starting point, but as with other ad platforms, you still must adjust your strategy based on your target audience(s) as well as your genre.

As with the other ad platforms above, you should clearly outline expectations, discuss goals, and what your ROI and CPC/CPM goals are, as well as anything you've tried in the past that has/hasn't worked. Communication is a vital part of ads management, especially in the beginning of the relationship with your ads manager.

PART THREE

READER MAGNET SITES: BOOKFUNNEL, STORY ORIGIN AND OTHERS

Reader magnets and associated sites are their own beasts and can be an excellent task to assign to your assistant.

There are several reader magnet sites. Each have their advantages and disadvantages. You may choose to use one or several and have your assistant book promotions through them.

ADD NEW READER MAGNETS OR BOOKS FOR SALE INTO THE SYSTEM AND SET UP LANDING PAGES FOR THEM

Whether you are setting up your reader magnets for the first time with a site, or if you're adding a new story to your available reader magnets, letting your assistant take the files and get the book set up, followed by creating the landing pages is an excellent task for them.

There are multiple things they can handle once that step has been collected:

- Setting up the landing page for gathering email addresses in various newsletter promotions.
- Setting up a landing page to allow readers already on your mailing list to get the new story.
- Setting up a landing page for other targets as well, such as A/B testing, visits or page interactions.

They can do the same thing for books that are on sale or in Kindle Unlimited that you wish to promote through discounted sales, as well as pages for books you might sell on your website, or for audiobooks (depending on the site).

Taking care of these things allows you or your assistant to sign up for various promotions for your mailing list and book sales.

SIGN UP FOR VARIOUS FREE BOOK GIVEAWAYS FOR NEWSLETTER PROMOS

Going through the multitude of promotions, especially on multiple sites, can be a time-consuming task (I know! I have done it often myself).

Finding out which promotional services accept what, making sure your magnet(s) are an appropriate fit for the promo and scheduling share dates that coordinate with when your newsletter goes out are appropriate tasks for an assistant.

Be sure they know when your newsletters go out and have a way for them to let you know what promotions need to be shared (unless they are handling the newsletter for you.)

SCHEDULE BOOK SALES PROMOTIONS

Most of the reader magnet sites also have book sale promotions. Some are for Kindle Unlimited, some are wide, some are for 99 cent books, and some are for other promotions. Whatever the promotion is, letting your assistant set these up for you frees up your time.

Like booking newsletter sign up promotions, there is a lot of searching and verification to make sure you're putting the book into the right promotions.

And, like in the previous section, be sure your assistant knows when your newsletters go out so they can schedule them appropriately within promotions. This will make sure your Bookfunnel stats stay good. In addition, be sure your assistant has a way to let you know what promotions need to be shared and when (unless they are handling the newsletter for you.)

SET UP PROMOS ON YOUR BEHALF FOR NEWSLETTER SIGN UPS OR BOOK SALES

Some authors like setting up newsletter sign up promotions or book sales promotions for other authors to participate in. If this is something you do regularly, or would you like to try, you can have your assistant can create and manage those for you as well.

Once again, you will need to communicate how often you want them run, duration, themes (if any), special requirements (if any), and any other requirements (genre, sales type, etc.).

Creating graphics, sharing the promotion in various groups to gain participants, approving participants, and verifying participants activity and choosing to allow them to be in future ones or not, as well as sharing the promotion once it is live are all useful tasks for an assistant to take on.

Deciding on themes for upcoming promotions for months ahead of time so you do not have to discuss it every month, assuming you want to do monthly promotions, might be a good decision. You may also decide to the same theme across multiple promotions: newsletter, Kindle Unlimited, and sales promos.

Yay may also have your assistant run closed promos where you select to have them email people you've worked with in the past to take part in the promotions.

Whatever you decide to do, be sure to communicate schedules and expectations to your assistant.

SET UP/PARTICIPATE IN NEWSLETTER SWAP OPPORTUNITIES AND BOOK THEM

Both Bookfunnel and Story Origin allow you to arrange newsletter swaps for your books, as well as those of your swap partner. As long as your assistant knows what genres/types of books you are looking to swap with, it is fairly easy for them to set it up.

Then they either need to let you know what is being shared when or mark it down for themselves to share in your newsletter on the appropriate date(s).

SHARE PROMOS ON SOCIAL MEDIA
AND NEWSLETTER

And last but not least, they can share promotions they have scheduled you to participate in on your social media platforms and your newsletter.

Many promoters require that shares happen before the midway point of the promotion or you'll be removed. Sharing on social media is a great way to make it happen if your newsletter is sent out after that point in the promotion.

PART FOUR

BOOK PUBLICATION

While some authors would be thrilled at the prospect of not having to deal with all the administrative side of uploading books, there is a word of caution. Amazon strongly frowns upon sharing your account with other people. You should also frown upon sharing your account username and password with anyone—even through a secure system like LastPass.

The reason for this is you are putting your Amazon account—and especially your Amazon account—at risk by allowing someone else login. If your assistant has been banned from their own KDP account in the past—and they do not inform you of this—you risk losing your account because Amazon may see their access of your account as violating their terms. Some people might not be forthcoming with about their account being banned, thinking it may not affect you or not wanting to lose out on work because they lost their account. However, even if they have not been banned, giving your asssistant access to your account still violates Amazon's Terms of Service.

As with other services where passwords are shared (without a

LastPass type program), you also risk your account being compromised if they are hacked or if they get upset and decide to take your account from you. If your KDP account is compromised, you will lose valuable time and money trying to get it back—*if* you get it back.

This is also risk with distribution sites such as Smashwords and Draft2Digital that will push your publication to all platforms. If you are going to share your account to allow your assistant to help with publication tasks, I can't urge you enough to invest in a program that allows you to grant and revoke access to your accounts instead of changing passwords.

All of that said, if you are interested in your assistant helping with pre-publication, publication, and post publication tasks, there are plenty of tasks they can do. Several of those tasks do not even require them needing access to your accounts and can save you a huge amount of time.

PUBLICATION CALENDAR MAINTENANCE

Maintaining a publication calendar is an important part of an assistant's tasks.

Book release dates and preorder deadlines can be added to a calendar. Some other items they could add and maintain for you include:

- Cover deadlines
- How far in advance the preorder will be scheduled
- Editing deadlines (can include when it needs to get to the editor, when it is supposed to come back, when it goes to proofreader, etc.)
- When final changes need to be completed
- When formatting needs to be done
- When to book promotions (if any)
- When the final upload for preorders is
- When to reach out for newsletter swaps (if any)

There are probably other things that could go on a calendar

that I'm not thinking of (like when to book an editor/cover artist/ etc.) for the next book.

Whatever your assistant needs to keep track of and remind you of or do themselves, it would be good for them to know and put in the calendar or have access to your calendar if you add dates in yourself.

BLURB WRITING—FIRST DRAFT OR COMPLETE

Many authors, including myself, hate writing blurbs, but some folks are fantastic at it or can get great at it. Blurb writing can be done a few different ways.

First, you need to decide how you want your assistant to get the information needed for the blurb. Do you write an outline or beats for the story they can reference? Do you want to give them the major points you want to hit and let them write from there? Or do you want them to read the book and then write it?

Once that's decided, figure out if you're going to review every blurb they come up with and revise it, or just a few and once they have it figured out, go from there.

Of course, if blurb writing is not up to your main assistant's workload, there are plenty of blurb writing specialists out there you can outsource it to, too.

CATEGORIES

Determining what categories would work best for your upcoming publication, especially if you're chasing orange tags on Amazon, can be a time-consuming task, especially if your novels are not always in the same categories. Using Publisher Rocket or looking at what categories similar books are in is something your assistant can do. You may review their category choices the first few times, but once it seems down pat, let them go for it.

Remember to ask them to search for 10 categories for each series.

KEYWORDS

Researching keywords for KDP (different from AMS keywords) are another task that an assistant can take on.

Once they know what the book is about and some base keywords for your book, they can research the best ones to be added to your metadata. You may review it the first few times for new series, then let them go for it.

Note: I advise using the same keywords and categories for all books in a series unless something huge would make a significant change later in the series for keywords or categories.

VERIFYING WHAT CATEGORIES AMAZON PLACED YOU IN, THEN CREATE/SUBMIT LETTERS TO ADD/REMOVE CATEGORIES

This task, by far, is important and many authors forget to do it. You can request up to ten categories via the help menu for your book, but sometimes Amazon does not put them in there or they add additional categories to books that they do not belong in.

Having your assistant check your backlist if you have never done this, as well as checking current releases to make sure they are in the right categories, is an important step. They can then craft messages for the book(s) to request removal from categories and additions to other categories.

Your assistant can request several books at once in their message if they need to be removed from/added to the same categories. It reduces the time needed for you to request them to be corrected if they have everything ready for you to tackle it.

They should then check in a week to make sure they are in the correct categories requested and repeat the process if it did not happen.

FORMATTING

Anyone who has formatted a book knows just how long it can take to get all the parts put together correctly and looking good.

If you normally format yourself with Vellum or Atticus, you can ask your assistant to do it if they have the programs or capabilities to format with a Word document.

There are a variety of ways to format a book. Some people use InDesign or Pages. Others use Vellum if they have a Mac or use MacinCloud. Or they may have invested in the new online publishing app, Atticus, which is usable on PC or Mac. Or they may use the Word document templates you can download from Amazon for formatting.

Make sure your assistant has everything needed to format the book and know what your preferences are for chapter headings, section breaks, etc. This task could eliminate hours of work from your plate if your assistant can handle it.

SET UP, UPLOAD, AND SUBMIT BOOKS TO AMAZON AND OTHER PLATFORMS

This is the first of two sections where sharing your username and password comes into play for your Amazon, wide distribution or wide platform accounts. Whether you set them up individually or use a distribution platform to send your book to multiple sales platforms, it takes time—admittedly far less time if you are using a site like Draft2Digital or Smashwords—but it still takes time. It takes even more time if you are using KDP and Ingram for your paperbacks and/or hardcover books.

However, this is an area where trust and several legal issues come into play.

I am not a lawyer and this IS NOT legal advice. However, if you shared your password and access to your account with your assistant(s), it is good to keep in mind doing so is technically against the terms of service of many of the platforms. If you are intent on doing so, there are many parts of this process your assistant can help with.

Whether you want them to set the book up from start to finish, just upload your files when they're ready and before preorder time runs out, update keywords, pull reports for preorders, or something else, there are plenty of tasks for them to take on.

Those tasks are even more numerous if you are submitting to each individual sales platform instead of via a distribution platform.

Be sure to discuss what you want them to do and if they are comfortable logging into your accounts and doing things on your behalf. If they are not comfortable with it, it should not, by any means, be a no-go for using them as an assistant. Chances are they are looking out for the safety of your accounts and their own in the future.

CORRECTING REPORTED KDP ERRORS

This task could be completed one of two ways. The first is for them to login to the account, look at the reported errors, make the corrections in the formatted version of the manuscript, upload the new version, then mark the changes either as completed or ignored.

The other option is to forward them the emails you receive from Amazon with the errors and have them change it from there. Your assistant lets you know when the manuscript is done and then you handle the upload and marking everything.

If you have a boxed set out, they would have to change both manuscripts.

You could also send them any corrections you receive from readers to correct.

Like the previous tasks, discuss with them what they will do and go from there.

CORRECT READER REPORTED ERRORS

Many authors request readers submit errors they find in published books directly to them instead of going through Amazon's reporting system due to how Amazon penalizes authors for said reports.

If you have a system set up for readers to report errors to you, you might have your assistant go through, verify the changes are legitimate, track those changes and make them in the manuscript(s), recreate the files and give it to you to upload to Amazon.

It is important that your assistant have a good understanding of grammar and spelling, how to make the changes in a document, and how to track what changes they've made so they do not go back in repeatedly to make the same changes when someone else reports it. They also need to tell when a change is a personal preference for wording from a reader and when it is a legitimate concern. For example, people will often tell you to spell out contractions or not use certain dialect phrases because it is not proper English, but it is how people speak. If they are not sure, they should confirm changes with you.

PART FIVE

BOOK SALES PROMOTIONS

One of the most time-consuming tasks, after social media scheduling and maintenance, is booking newsletter promotion sites. It may not seem complicated, but often there's rewriting of blurbs to meet site requirements, filling out all the forms, etc. An assistant can work with you to figure out which books to promote each month, then schedule them out. They can also help with other tasks associated with promoting your new releases and backlist.

CREATING A PROMOTION CALENDAR

If you have multiple series and a plan for promoting your books each quarter, or year, creating and maintaining a promotion calendar so that you and your assistant know what's on promotion when in order to book promotions, reduce prices/set up Kindle Countdown Deals/Free Promotions, reach out for newsletter swaps and more is an important task your assistant can take on.

These calendars could be in Google Calendar, iCal, or a special spreadsheet where you track things for each month. It all depends on what works for you and your assistant.

Creating the calendar will require communication from you regarding when you want your promotions done. As the author, you are the primary strategist for your business, but your assistant can help you execute that promotional strategy.

For example, if you promote the first book in a series with every new release or every few months, it is important for them to know to add it to the calendar. If you have an extensive backlist and you want them to rotate through promoting first books in series each month or multiple times a month, they need to know so they can create a schedule.

The calendar can also include information such as when they applied for BookBub Featured deals with specific books and when they can apply for them again. Also, special group promotions they sign up for in Bookfunnel that coincides with paid promotions.

Ideally, both you and your assistant could add and update items on the calendar, but it would be important for each to communicate with the other if something has changed without warning—for example, you are including a book in a group sales effort and are changing promotion dates from normal to that specific date so that they can book accordingly or change dates if they already booked them.

The promotions calendar plays into many other tasks below that an assistant can take on when booking promotions. Note: further down, I discuss ReaderLinks. One option available within ReaderLinks is the AuthorPlanner which can be used for planning promotions and adding in notes for each promotion site, tasks for new book launches, and more.

LOTS OF PAID SITES TO APPLY TO/BOOK AND MANY NEED TO BE BOOKED WEEKS, IF NOT MONTHS OUT.

The biggest task an assistant can take on is booking newsletter promotion sites. While some can be booked at the last minute, many cannot. Some, for example, need to be booked two months out, like Robin Reads, eReader Cafe and Book Barbarian. Others I would suggest to look at, based on the sale price of the book is Bargain Booksy, FreeBooksy, and Red Feather Romance.

Other promotion sites should be booked a month ahead of time, such as eReader News Today, Kindle Nation Daily and My Book Cave. Some can only be booked, at max, three weeks to a month out, based on their requirements.

I book a lot of promotions and I book them in bulk, especially when I have discount codes to use. Your assistant should plan on spending time each month booking what they can two months out, then booking other sites closer to the promotion as well.

Knowing what they booked and when the promotions happen should be a part of this. Personally, I have a spreadsheet that shows what promotion sites are booked on which dates. You may have a specific order you like your promotions to be booked in. For example, you may want the sites you know generate more sales at the end of your promotion period and other sites at the beginning. Or you may have promotions you want before and after a BookBub featured deal.

There may be some sites that your books just do not get a good return on investment from. Let them know not to use those sites or to test those sites every few months to see if the ROI has improved.

Something to consider—will you have them paying through your PayPal/Credit Card, or will you want them to pay for it on their account, then invoice you for the costs when done? There is no right or wrong answer to this and it all depends on what you, and they, have available. They may not have the financial capacity to front the costs and there is nothing wrong with that. Work it out with them how you want it to be paid for. If you do set up a 'slush fund' or advertising account they have access to, have your assistant keep a basic accounting sheet to show how the money is being spent and where.

VERIFY PROMOS RAN AND TRACK SALES

It is always important to make sure the promotions you have paid for actually run when your book is on sale.

Your assistant can take on this task by signing up to receive the newsletters on the various promotion sites. They can then check those newsletters on the day reserved for the promotion.

They can also check the websites sand social media where appropriate for promotions.

When promotions are missed (and that does occasionally happen), they can reach out to the promotion site and see if they can run it on their next available date or request a refund. Most sites are extremely good at making good when errors like these occur.

It is also good to make sure they used the right cover or the right link. There are a few sites who you may submit a different book and they promote the previous one that was in the system. For example, if you had a partial boxed set then resubmitted a complete boxed set, they may promote the previous boxed set instead of the current. Or if you added content and republished with a new ASIN, they may use the old link, not realizing it because it was in their system. I have also seen instances where you may have updated a cover where they use the previously submitted cover instead of the new one. These are all situations where your assistant can reach out to them to see if they have a way to correct the situation and make it right.

I always believe it is a good thing to verify promotions actually happen: that way, if there's an abnormality in sales during a promotion week (you get fewer sales than expected, or more sales than expected), you can look at what promotions happened when and figure out why.

ANALYZE RETURN ON INVESTMENT AND READ THROUGH

Knowing what newsletter promotion sites work well for your genre and books is important. If you are not sure, the best way to do this is to have your assistant look at sales numbers for the book in question, then check the sell-through to the rest of the series. They can look at numbers sold and page reads each day to see how the promotions did (even though page reads will increase after the event).

Determining if promotion sites worked for you to use in the future can save time and money down the road for you and your assistant.

It is important to note that some folks may not buy the book from the promotion sites and either put them into KU to read at a later time, or bookmark it for later. Often you will not see a spike in page reads for a week or more after the promotion, so disregarding sites as ineffective based on sales alone might not be a good idea.

It is also important to note that while some sites may be great for a while, their ROI may decrease. And the reverse is true as well. A site may have had horrible ROI, but now has good return.

It is always a good idea to test sites that did poorly in the past to see how they do in the future. It is also possible that some books may do better than others on those sites, so you can't just write them off completely.

There are also new sites popping up from time to time. It does not hurt to try them as well and see how they do, especially as they grow and add more subscribers.

STACKING PROMOTIONS

Rarely do you book just one promotion site for your books and nothing more. Stacking promotions over a period of a week or two weeks is a great way to build sales and take advantage of the period when your book is on sale to get more eyes on it.

As mentioned in the section regarding booking sites, you will want to let them know if you have any specific way you want your promotions stacked or order to promote through the time during which the price will be reduced.

Stacking paid newsletter promotions is just one way to promote books. Coordinating those promotions with social media posts, newsletter swaps, Facebook or Amazon ads, and promotion in other groups are other tasks your assistant can add to their to-do list for the promotion of the book. If you have another assistant handling Facebook/Amazon ads, coordinate with them (or have them connected to the promotion calendar), so they can coordinate ads appropriately.

Newsletter Swaps and putting the book into sales promotions on Bookfunnel or Story Origin for the time they are on sale can also help.

Discuss what additional tasks you want them to do for the promotion period and let them work from there.

PART SIX

GRAPHICS

Creating graphics is a time-consuming process, no matter what program you use. Whether you have a subscription to BookBrush you want your assistant to use, or if they know how to use and have a subscription to Photoshop or have downloaded GIMP or purchased AffinityPhoto or some other free or paid for app, having your assistant take on creating graphics would be a good use of time—assuming they have the skill and eye for it.

There are many free downloadable templates for books, tablets and more if they use Photoshop or a program that can open .psd files. These are excellent for creating unique promotion graphics.

Be sure your assistant can acquire, or you acquire for them, any specific fonts needed for branding. You may need to pay for some fonts, and your assistant must be conscious as to whether they are using fonts that are free for commercial use or not. If you use fonts that are not free for commercial use and you have not bought the correct license, you may have to compensate the font creators down the road. The same goes for stock images, photographs, etc.

PROMOTIONAL GRAPHICS FOR LAUNCH, SALES, SEASONAL, ETC.

If your assistant has the programs and artistic ability to create various promotional graphics for your social media and website, this is a great time saver—especially if you have multiple graphics to create for each book launch.

Not only can you create graphics for book launches, but you can also create your own branded memes, custom seasonal graphics, sales graphic, reading order graphics (or updating them) and more.

In addition, many authors have taken to creating timelines for their universe. Some have created family trees, character cards, creature cards and more as bonus content for their fans. They can also create flyers, buttons, postcards, table and wall banners, and other promotional materials for in person events.

Graphics take time, though, especially if you want custom graphics regularly.

SERIES PROMO GRAPHICS

Once a series has several books out, or is complete, it is a good idea to create series promotion graphics. Having different ones available, especially for seasonal or special promotions, are great to have on hand.

When your assistant knows what you want for graphics, they can set about creating them and adding to them as you add series or books to the individual series.

A+ GRAPHICS FOR AMAZON

With the launch of A+ graphics for books on Amazon, this would be a great thing for an assistant to handle, especially if you want to have some created for backlist series or new series launching soon.

Be sure to find some examples of A+ graphics you like on Amazon for them to look at so they have something to work from. Make sure they know what slogan/types of graphics you want and any important branding elements and let them work from there. They can find all the dimensions needed for graphics on Amazon and work to design what looks best for the main series page and for subpages.

Once approved, if they have access to your Amazon account, they can upload everything for the A+ content. Otherwise, you can do it and request any tweaks necessary to make it look amazing.

OTHER

There are quite a few other graphics that could be created and changed out each year. Those include, but are definitely not limited to: banner graphics for Twitter, Facebook pages and groups; graphics for other social media platforms, and website header images where appropriate. You may also want individual books mocked up as paperbacks, hardbacks, ebook, etc. on different backgrounds.

If you are inclined to run your own Bookfunnel or Story Origin promotions, creating appropriate graphics for the promotion banner and for participants to use would be a good use of an assistant's capabilities.

They could also create branded "This or That" type graphics for social media, branded question memes, and more.

Brainstorm ideas for future projects with your assistant from time to time, that way if either of you have new ideas, you can bounce them off each other!

PART SEVEN

NEWSLETTER

Whether you send out a newsletter weekly, biweekly, monthly, or sporadically, all the parts involved in sending out a newsletter are time-consuming.

The good news is that most of the major email marketing platforms (MailChimp, Mailerlite, ActiveCampaign, etc.) provide you with the ability to add users to your account so your assistant can do things on your behalf without sharing your username or password. Not all email marketing platforms provide this extra access ability, so you will have to decide ahead of time if you are going to share your account information with your assistant and how.

Discuss which of the following potential tasks your assistant would take on, that you will give up, then work with them from there.

WRITING AND SENDING OUT NEWSLETTERS

The more often you send out a newsletter, the more time-consuming it can be to prepare the newsletter to send out.

Whether you write the initial message and let your assistant format the newsletter with your content, or you have them write the newsletter themselves, it can save a great deal of time. If you have multiple books or Bookfunnel-type promotions to share, ads or other content to add to each newsletter, it can take even more time.

Decide which method you would prefer, keeping in mind you can always change a newsletter before it goes out—especially if you want to write a special note to send out or if you want to send out a special email on a different day.

Be sure to review the frequency you send out newsletters, writing style, potential topics, etc., when setting them up to take this task on.

BUILDING YOUR LIST

An important task for an author is growing their mailing list. While some of the previous tasks (like Bookfunnel/StoryOrigin/related contests) are all parts of this, there are other things they can do to help grow your mailing list.

If you are running ads directing people to your website, your assistant could come up with copy to encourage them to sign up for the newsletter while sending them directly to the newsletter page on your website. They may also do social media posts encouraging people to join your mailing list.

There is also making sure a link to your newsletter sign up page is in your backmatter for all of your books. There may be other methods you and your assistant come up with to try, as things change fast in the social media world.

LIST CLEAN UP

If you are an author who regularly cleans and optimizes your mailing list, you know just how time-consuming this task can be—especially if you do reengagement campaigns before going through the process.

If you decide for your assistant to do this, be sure to review the following with them:

- How you determine who gets targeted for list reengagement
- How many emails are in the system that need to go through
- What type of engagement you are looking for to keep the person on your list
- How long after the last email until they are put into the sequence for removal

Of course, you may already have an automation sequence that handles all steps of this that need to be triggered very quarter or however often you want to have your list optimized by your assistant. Either way, it is one less thing you would have to deal with.

SETTING UP AUTOMATION SEQUENCES AS NEEDED

Whether you are setting up your first automation sequence or others as your needs grow, allowing your assistant to set those up for you would be a time saver.

For example, if you wanted a different automation sequence depending on where the contact entered your list—website, Bookfunnel, contest, or another way—this would be something the assistant could do. Or if you sell stuff on your website and you need a recapture sales automation. Needs for different automations sequence will grow as your author career grows.

Of course, you would have to discuss the details of any sequences or specific triggers you want in the sequence(s), what the sequence is for, potentially review the copy if it is for something unique, and go from there.

An important reminder: not every newsletter platform provides the same options for automation sequences. If you've changed newsletter providers recently, keep this in mind for changes that might be necessary when setting up new automations.

MOVING PROVIDERS (IF DECIDED TO DO SO)

If you decide to change providers, there's a lot of work that goes into it.

Often, it involves not just moving over your lists, but also setting up forms you use on your website and elsewhere, recreating all automation sequences, setting up tags, as well as re-syncing all the sites that are tied to the email system, setting up email templates, and more. I have done this specific task twice since I started being an assistant in 2019. I can safely tell you, it is a lot of work.

Making sure you have a task list for everything that needs to be moved over, broken out with who is doing what (or if your assistant is doing all of it), discuss a deadline for moving over and sending out the first newsletter, and discuss when you plan to end the previous service payment plan.

This would also include updating your backmatter in your books if you send a subscriber directly to a landing page instead of a page on your website. If you are moving and this was how you previously had it set up, you might strongly consider changing the link to one on your website for two reasons. First, it drives traffic to your website. Second, if you change providers in the future, you do not have to worry about going through all of your backmatter and updating it again.

NOTE: This task WILL take longer than you expect it to, especially if neither of you are familiar with the new system you are migrating to. You will learn many new methods for the new system, which may mean redoing things as well.

ADDITIONAL NOTE: I strongly recommend giving yourself at least a month or two on the old system to make sure you've hit every place that links to your email sign up and email system to make sure everything is going to the right place.

ROUTINE CHECKS TO MAKE SURE SUBSCRIBERS PROGRESS THROUGH AUTOMATION SEQUENCES, WHY USERS UNSUBSCRIBE, ETC.

I have encountered situations where various newsletter programs do not always work as intended. This is often seen by users not progressing through automation sequences, never receiving a single email from your automaton sequence, and never moving into your main mailing list to start receiving regular emails from you. You will not know this unless you check your automation sequences to make sure that people move through them.

Checking these every couple of months is a good idea, that way you can remove them from the sequence and re-add them to that sequence or a new sequence letting them know they never progressed through and you hope they stay. This is a good task to assign to an assistant as it takes a bit of time and tracking and would be better suited to someone who can do it on a scheduled basis however often you want them to do it.

Another thing to consider is seeing the unsubscribe reasons. Keep in mind, many just unsubscribe and choose "too many emails" after they get one email. But see if there are other reasons in the list that you can address to prevent future unsubscribes.

BACKING UP LISTS

When was the last time you backed up your mailing list, including your unsubscribes, bounces, and everything else?

Hint: It is probably not as often as it should be done.

With cyber-attacks increasing, it is always a good idea to keep copies of your mailing list on hand, if not monthly, at least once a quarter. Keeping multiple backups is not a bad idea. Online in a cloud backup like Dropbox, OneDrive or Google Drive is a good idea, but also having one that you update on an external drive or flash drive is a good idea too—just in case something catastrophic happens.

Allowing your assistant to be responsible for those backups and putting them in a shared Dropbox or other cloud service where you can create a folder just for backups. Be sure to keep a couple of them. That way you have something to revert to just in case a file corrupts or something else goes wrong.

PROCESSING UNSUBSCRIBE REQUESTS THAT COME AS REPLIES TO YOUR NEWSLETTER

While you are required to have an unsubscribe link on your newsletter, some people either miss it or just do not care to look for it and go through the process to unsubscribe.

Most people do not know, but you are required to remove them within 10 days of receiving the unsubscribe request and yes, you must comply with the request although they can just as easily do it themselves.

You could just forward the emails to your assistant, have them unsubscribe the individual and let you know they have been removed so you can reply to them and inform them their request to unsubscribe has been processed.

Then you are within the letter of the law, and you have one less task to tackle.

PART EIGHT

NEWSLETTER SWAPS

Arranging and scheduling newsletter swaps is an important part of growing your author business. While there are many groups and many ways to go about arranging a swap, it remains a time-consuming part of the business.

There are really only two tasks associated with newsletter swaps, which will be covered in the following sections:

1. Scheduling them with other authors

2. Making sure your books show up when they are supposed in the other authors' newsletters.

SCHEDULING SWAPS WITH OTHER AUTHORS

If your assistant knows how often your newsletter goes out, when it goes out, any list size limitations, and how many books you want to put in a single newsletter, they can seek newsletter swaps and schedule them on your behalf. Arranging, scheduling, and making sure promised swaps have happened are a common task assigned to assistants.

There are many ways an assistant can arrange newsletter swaps. How they do them, or if you leave it up to them decide, is an important thing to decide.

Several things should be relayed to an assistant before they schedule swaps:

- When you would like to arrange swaps (every time a new book releases, just when the first book in a series is released, when a book goes on sale, free swaps, etc.)
- List size limitations (i.e. You would prefer to swap with a list between a certain size range or over a certain size range, or you do not care about size range because every author has to start out somewhere)

- Number of books you want to put in each newsletter
- Sites you want them to use (Story Origin, Bookfunnel, other)
- Facebook groups you want them to use (besides others they may know of)
- Authors you want them to reach out to specifically either via email or social media for swaps
- Authors you do NOT want them to swap with
- Your typical newsletter schedule (be sure to let them know if you are adding dates or removing some ahead of time so they can schedule accordingly)
- Do you use Google Forms or something else to help arrange swaps? If so, do you want them to use that as well or can they do it on their own through their account? Or do you do something else?
- Anything else you think they need to know

You may want your assistant to maintain a calendar (via Google, iCal, etc.) for you to know what books are supposed to appear when. Alternatively, use a spreadsheet so you can see what you are sharing when and what they are sharing of yours and when. Or for them to know when they are sharing it if they do your newsletters for you.

They also need to track any swaps you may receive direct requests for. Many times, authors who are interested in swapping with another author in their genre will attempt to contact the author directly through their website or Facebook, not knowing you have an assistant that handles all of it. You can forward any email requests to your assistant for them to reach out, or connect them on Facebook, whatever is easiest for you, so things do not slip through the cracks.

MAKING SURE SWAPS APPEAR IN AUTHOR'S NEWSLETTER AND NEWSLETTER THEY SIGNED UP FOR

It is often a good idea to ask for links to the newsletter your book is supposed to appear in or for someone to subscribe to another author's newsletter to verify that your book(s) appear when they are supposed to.

While it is rare that someone will miss their share date, it does happen, and it offers an opportunity to reach out to them and see if they will share on another date or share on social media or something else instead.

It does not take a lot of time to check the newsletters, but it is something that an assistant could take on.

PART NINE

SETTING UP/MAINTAINING READERLINKS, BOOKS2READ, GENIUS LINKS

Whether it is the first time setting up a link service such as ReaderLinks, Genius Links, Pretty Links, Books2Read or similar, or if you are just needing links to be created whenever you have a new release, this is a task they can take on.

Each link generating site has different capabilities, which will determine how much work this is for your assistant.

The following sections will discuss ReaderLinks tasks more than other tasks.

READERLINKS

If you are new to Readerlinks or do not have everything set up/maintained, your assistant can help with this.

If you have an extensive backlist, setting up Readerlinks can be time-consuming, especially if you are just setting it up for the first time. Maintaining it can take a couple hours a week, especially if they are managing reader teams, organizing their feedback, uploading sales content, and analyzing data.

If you are familiar with ReaderLinks, the rest of this section will not matter a lot to you. If you are unfamiliar with it, continue reading the next few paragraphs.

Readerlinks is a multi-functional author management platform. Not only does it provide universal links with affiliate codes for your books, but also direct links to your review pages to encourage reviews, audiobook links, paperbacks and more. You can add as many custom links to the books as you like, so you do not have to add them if you want to track link clicks. Some custom links I have added include specific links for each social media platform I have, websites, book backmatter, links for ads and more.

You can upload reports from KDP into ReaderLinks to get

analytics on read through, statistics for ads, CTR analysis, and much more.

You can let people apply for ARC team/reader groups through the site, monitor corrections suggested, as well as links to reviews that they create. They can even copy and paste reviews into the system for ease of verification. An ARC team can be created for each book and you can set up different options for them as well as automation of certain processes.

If you have not checked out all the things ReaderLinks can do for you, I strongly suggest visiting the site because I could do an entire book based on this amazing product alone.

The nice thing about ReaderLinks is that your assistant can create their own account, then be granted access to your account to manage everything. You can also accept applications to be your assistant through the system. You just have to turn that option on.

ADDING BOOKS

Adding books and series into ReaderLinks does not take a lot of time, but it does take time.

If you are setting up ReaderLinks for the first time and want to get your backlist populated into the system, allowing your assistant to login on your account and add all the series and books will help. Once set up, all they have to do is add new books as you have them available. You can add books in without an ASIN. If you have a cover already available, you can add that to the app or just put the books in as placeholders until the ASINs are available. This will allow it to be set up without you spending a lot of time adding your backlist and new books to it.

I also use the system to store my upcoming title names when I have them before I have the covers. That way, they are all in one place.

MANAGING READER TEAMS THROUGH READERLINKS

Readerlinks provides an all-in-one system for reader teams which includes applying for books, automatically approving people who you will allow for any book, declining others, tracking suggested changes and tracking reviews that members of the reader team put into the system. You can use it for every book in a series, or just selected books.

There are some steps involved in setting up books for reader teams and managing them, but they are all things your assistant can handle. Provide them with the information needed for setting up each book, including but not limited to the number of chapters in the book, book download link unless the assistant is creating it for you, what you expect of the reader team, what they will get, and any additional information that they would need to relay to the team members for each book. You will also want to let them know how long of a period they have to get any suggested changes and reviews done. If you have questions for your reader team, be sure to let your assistant know what those are so they can include them in the Reader Team set up.

It is important to note that you have to turn off applications to the team manually and turn on/off the activity level of the team once the book is out. Otherwise, you will continue to get applications once you're done with the launch.

UPLOADING OTHER CONTENT

ReaderLinks provides you with tools to analyze sales connected to advertising and read through. In order for those tools to work correctly, you must upload reports from Amazon KDP and your Amazon Ad account, as well as manually inputting other income and expenses for the book so you can see your return on investments.

If you export reports regularly and want your assistant to upload them and run the ReaderLink reports, that is something they could easily do on your behalf.

SETTING UP EXTRA LINKS

A benefit to ReaderLinks is you can easily create links for all of your books just once by adding them into the system. While it comes with default links built in, you may want specific links for Pinterest, TikTok, or sharing in promotions. Or if you need links for special promotions in Bookfunnel or elsewhere where you want to track the clicks you get to the links, you can create links for those specific books too.

I like ReaderLinks because I can specify whether I want affiliate codes to be used for a new link when it is created, which can come in handy if you provide someone with a ReaderLinks link for a newsletter swap. This is something to keep in mind if you want to see how many clicks you get in a swap (assuming they use the link provided).

GENIUS LINKS

Another great universal link tool is Genius Links (geniuslink.com). Like Readerlinks, it requires a fee to use, but it provides additional options as well. You can create folders for links that you can use to sort where the links are at, if they use affiliate links, and more.

If you have no universal links set up for your books and have decided which company you are going to go with, your assistant can go through and create the links and put them where they belong to transition to a universal link service. You may create a spreadsheet for the links if you create different links for multiple uses.

BOOKS2READ

Similar to ReaderLinks and Genius Links, Books2Read is another site that can create universal links for your books.

The upside to Books2Read, which is run by Draft2Digital, is that it is a FREE service and it links not just to Amazon, but if you are wide, it will link to your book at those sites as well. It also pulls links in for paperback and audiobooks. You can easily search your account for links you have already created and use them again. They also allow you to create custom names for the links besides the random numbers and letters they assign to each link they create. They also allow you to curate reading lists to share with your readers.

The downside (and it is not a big one), is that if you want a set of links for newsletters without affiliate codes and another set of links that have affiliate codes, you need to create two accounts because you can't have an account with both types of links in it. This is not a bad thing, you just have to remember which login is which when you want to create your links.

If you have not set up Books2Read already or decide to transition to it from a different universal link company, your assistant can take care of creating the links for you, provided you let them know any requirements for custom links, how many accounts you need, etc.

To make tracking of links easier, you may create a spreadsheet for the links if you have them creating them for multiple uses. That way they are easy to find with and without affiliate links.

PRETTY LINKS VIA YOUR WORDPRESS WEBSITE

Pretty Links is a great way to use your own website to create masked affiliate links or just plain links to your Amazon books.

Pretty Links is a premium WordPress plugin that makes it easy to shorten, cloak, share, and even track your affiliate links. This can be done from the WordPress dashboard, and with much more functionality than your average link shortener.

While there is a Pretty Links Lite version, the premium version offers a myriad of additional redirection types, conversion reports, and a wealth of automation and sharing tools to supercharge the way you present your site's links.

If you have a WordPress site and do not already have this set up but want to use it, this is something your assistant can take on. If you already have it set up, it is a task your assistant can add on to their list. They would just need to know what you want done and any specific instructions to create the links how you want them created.

OTHER SITES

There are several other sites out there that can create link shorteners or provide universal links for Amazon books. As the industry continues to grow, it will not be a surprise if additional sites pop up.

Consider these sites if you decide to change from what you are currently using or if one of these established sites go away. Transitioning from one service to another is time-consuming and would be a valuable use of your assistant's time and resources.

PART TEN

SOCIAL MEDIA

When I started outlining this book, I did an informal survey of 20 indie authors to see if I was on the right path. I asked them: "If you could farm out five tasks to an assistant, what would they be and why?" Every author included social media management in their answers, and for most of them, it was their number one answer.

It does not surprise me or anyone who has done any social media work at all—it is time-consuming. The more platforms you have, the more time it eats up. And while it will not completely remove social media from your hands—because, let's be honest, you're still going to do stuff on your personal social media and may still post stuff here and there on your author accounts—it will free up a lot of your time.

This section will cover several topics, including:

- Managing social media accounts
- Tools for scheduling
- Social media calendars
- Branding

- Graphics
- Swaps

But before we talk about those things, I think talking about social media itself is important.

Whether you have one social media account, several or are adding a new platform to your platform, remember that the most important part of social media is interaction and engagement. If you have no or few social media accounts, I can't stress "start out small" enough. There are so many platforms out there, even with an assistant, you (and possibly they) will get overwhelmed trying to get things set up and going.

That being said, having a Facebook page for your author name or pen name is crucial, especially if you plan to do Facebook ads (and if you are not considering that, why are not you?). Many will say a Facebook group is also essential and I agree with that. You can share from your page to your group and get more interactions with the post that is on your page. The more engagement, the more it gets seen organically.

But it is also important to remember that your fans also want to get to know you and see some personal things from you as an author. Whether you're sharing pictures of your pets, fun things you're doing, a look into your day, pictures of an outing you are at or something else, even with an assistant, it is important to share them.

Now, you could share them on one platform and your assistant could pull the images and share them on the other platforms. Or you could share them with the platforms and let the admin handle marketing, fan interaction, comments, etc.

How much or how little you want your assistant to do is something you will have to determine.

You will also want to have a discussion with them and see what platforms they're interested in taking on or starting from scratch if you want to expand. You may have an assistant who has some really great ideas for TikTok, Clubhouse or whatever the next hot social media trend is. Listen to their ideas. You do not have to try them all and may decide to wait a bit before adding another platform under your belt.

You will also have to find out if they are interested or able to do ads, if that is what you want to do and what you're going to be running ads for. Will it be for newsletter sign ups? Promotion of Book #1 in a series (or multiple series), your author website, merchandise? Or something else? Do you know your budget for ads? Are you willing to add them as an admin to your business ad account, or will they need to run ads from their account and invoice you?

The next thing to consider is access to your accounts. Protecting your passwords to your accounts is something I cannot emphasize enough, and there is an entire chapter regarding this. Some platforms, especially Facebook, you can grant people access to your account with their own account. What level of access they have is up to you, but I will give a warning on this.

Anyone with Admin status on your account CAN remove you as admin and take over your page. This is true with a malicious attack, but it is just as true if they get hacked and their account compromised or you get attacked and compromised. This recently happened to a popular, traditionally published author, and it took a week or more for them to regain access to the account.

I strongly encourage you as well as whomever accesses your account to have two-factor authentication turned on ALL the time. It helps protect your accounts more than you know. I also stress changing your password and making sure your password for social media is not used anywhere else.

Some accounts you can't give access to like this. You may invest in a social media scheduling platform where you can grant people access to schedule your posts on other platforms. Many of these accounts cost more to have additional users. Or you may have an account that you share with them with your platforms already established on it so you only share one password with them.

If you gave them access to your accounts, even if they are trustworthy, you run the risk if they become compromised because of a virus or are hacked/tricked into logging into a phishing site, you may still lose your account. Be prepared to retrieve your account and the time it will take to do so. It will not be easy and I can't guarantee you will get it back.

I preach a lot about security because I've seen too many accounts compromised in the past few years.

PART ONE

MANAGING ACCOUNTS

FACEBOOK PAGES

Whether you have one author page, a series page, or several pages, you will need to decide which page(s) you want your assistant to have access to. They have to be added to each one individually. If you have multiple assistants because of various genres, be sure to authorize them for the correct accounts.

For those that are not familiar with the settings for Facebook pages, you can assign the following roles to an assistant:

Admin: This level of access has the most power. They can add and remove other admin, editors, moderators, advertisers and analysts. They can change page settings and more. In addition, they can do everything the other roles can do, including but not limited to publishing, replying to, and moderating posts; sending Messenger messages as the page; respond to and delete comments on the page; post from Facebook to Instagram; create and adjust ads or boost posts; see which page user created a post or comment; and view insights. If an Instagram account is connected, an admin can respond to and delete comments, send direct messages, sync business contact info and create ads on Instagram.

Editor: This level of access is just below Admin and they can do almost everything as an admin except change page settings, add users to roles.

Moderator: This role can publish, reply to, and moderate posts. They can send Messenger messages as the page; respond to and delete comments on the page; see which page user created a post or comment; and view insights. If an Instagram account is connected, a moderator can respond to comments, send direct messages, and create ads.

Advertiser: If you have someone who specializes in Facebook ads but does not want to do any of the other related tasks, this is the role for them. They can create ads, see which page role created posts or commented on posts and view ads. This person could not respond as the page to comments on the ads, your other admins would need to do that.

Analyst: This type of role is appropriate for someone consulting to advise how to improve your social media reach or to interpret your insights. This role can see which admin created or commented on posts and can view insights. They can't do anything else.

Knowing what level of access you want your assistant to have is important. It is also important to note, even though I did not include it above, that a page admin/editor will also have access to moderate any fan group connected to the page. They will also be able to access any groups you have added the page to and interact as the page in those groups (which is great for takeovers). They can also use the page to reply on other pages.

Make sure your assistant knows what you are expecting from them for managing your page(s). Will they be scheduling posts only? Responding to questions on the page and via messenger? Do you want them monitoring comments and liking/responding to them? Do you want them to invite people who interact with the page to like the page? Will they be creating custom graphics and videos for it? Will they be doing ads?

Do you want them to check the page once a day? A few times during the day? Anytime they get notifications? Be sure they know what the expectations are before they agree to taking on page tasks.

Facebook is encouraging the use of hashtags again. Are you going to want them to research and use hashtags in posts? Do you have a specific series of hashtags you want them to use when posting?

Will you want them to participate in groups on your behalf and doing takeovers with your page to promote your books?

Will they participate in your group on your behalf with the page? Or will you want them to post as your assistant in the group? Or a mixture of both?

These are all things that are worth having a discussion about, along with other topics I may not have thought of, and checking with your assistant after a set amount of time to see how they're doing and anything new that can be done or changed.

FACEBOOK GROUPS

Groups, like pages, are an integral part of interacting with fans and building your fan base. Many authors have both a fan page and a group(s) to have better interactions with fans. Your assistant can be integral here with keeping things moving smoothly.

If your assistant has access to your page and your page is an admin of the group, your assistant can do some (or in some cases most), actions as the page (assuming they are a page admin instead of editor). Some tasks, however, can only be done as an admin of the group. I suggest making them a moderator/admin of the group as well as your page so they can do things under their own name as well.

One of the regular, time-consuming tasks, besides moderating posts and replying to comments, is approving or declining new users for the group. I always encourage group owners to have group questions set up for joining. Even with the changes to public groups, having questions to allow interaction in the group is important. If the answers for admittance to the group are not obvious, be sure the assistant knows what answers are acceptable to let people in.

Another thing is updating the cover image for the group. Typically speaking, only admins of the group can change the image, so if this is something you want them to do regularly, their account has to be admin. If they are not admin, even if the page is admin, it will not let them change the header image.

Much like the warning with Facebook pages, making someone an admin of a group is a risky proposition because they have the same amount of control you do. I'm not saying not to do it, just know the advantages and disadvantages of doing so.

INSTAGRAM

The nice thing about Instagram, which has changed in the recent couple of years, is you now can post to Instagram from your Facebook page and schedule posts with Facebook and other social media scheduling programs.

This has helped to eliminate one of the biggest challenges of posting to Instagram for many assistants. Ultimately, it means you do not have to share your password to your Instagram account with your assistant and it means your assistant does not have to switch accounts to post to your account.

It is a huge win—speaking as an assistant who would 'schedule via Hootsuite' just to be told by Hootsuite app to copy the post into Instagram after you made sure you were logged into the correct Instagram account and post it on the schedule—this change is a huge improvement.

Instagram has always been big for authors, but it has been growing more so of late, especially with Bookstagramers and influencers using it to build other brands.

However, like many platforms that use hashtags, stories and images, you have to do your research and change your strategy regularly to meet goals. You, as an author, can give the more personal side of things by posting action pictures, pet pictures, family pictures, etc. to your Instagram, and your assistant can help by making sure there is a mix of other things as well. Whether it is inspirational sayings, images of your books, mockups, character pictures or other images, there are many things they can do.

They can also research hashtags that are good for your genre and what should get more eyes on you and your platform. They could also research Bookstagramers and influencers and see what reach they have and if they would be worth reaching out to to feature your books.

Just like with Facebook, and through Facebook, they can view and reply to comments on Instagram posts or delete spam posts (you would be surprised how many of these can come through regularly). They can also respond to private messages where appropriate.

You might also consider having them routinely see what other authors in your genre are posting to come up with ideas for new posts for your account as well.

TWITTER

Many authors have a love-hate relationship with Twitter—and other social media accounts. Twitter creates a unique challenge for authors because of the character limit required. Despite the message limits, Twitter can be a good marketing tool for authors as it allows you to reach targeted audiences with hashtags and tagging accounts.

Twitter is one of the social media platforms that can be integrated into a scheduling platform you can give them access to so they do not have to share your Twitter account.

They can also research Twitter-specific hashtags and accounts to tag that are good for your genre and discover what should get more eyes on you and your platform.

You can also pay for ads on Twitter. That would be something you or your assistant would need to research and see if it is a worthwhile investment for your brand.

PINTEREST

Pinterest is a great way to share covers, graphics, and ads for your books, but like other social media platforms, it can be a time suck.

If you have a business Pinterest account, you can invite your assistant to manage your account through their Pinterest account. This allows them to administer your account as if they are you and makes it easier for them to manage everything without your password while allowing you to add things to it as well.

With the variety of boards and ability to share an infinite number of things to Pinterest, along with links to your releases, you can create quite an interactive following. You may have your assistant create a board for each series, posting the new releases to it along with preorder announcements, quotes, and more. Or you could have a mood board for your characters where you, and your assistant, post things related to the characters and the books.

They can also post to other shared Pinterest boards. Several authors run collaborative Pinterest boards for various genres to help with cross promotion of books.

Pinterest also has the ability to schedule pins, so if you want there to be regular pins showing up on your boards, your assistant can schedule those out as well.

Similar to Twitter and Instagram, hashtags play a huge role in the success of Pinterest. Your assistant can research Pinterest-specific hashtags that are good for your genre and discover what should get more eyes on you and your platform. They can also find shared boards to post your books to. Pinterest also has ads.

Pinterest can be a useful tool in your kit, but only if you communicate what your goals are with your assistant and both of you feel it is a worthwhile time investment.

TIKTOK

TikTok has become all the rage for authors lately. While you may want to do some videos (and most definitely should), other videos could be produced, or edited and uploaded, by your assistant.

And like other platforms, they could look for hashtags for you to use when you post videos based on your genre and what's popular on BookTok.

They could even talk with other authors to arrange hand-off videos with books in the same genre that all the authors could.

And, of course, similar to other platforms, they can respond to and moderate comments on videos.

As far as I know (as of January 20, 2021), there is no way to add an administrator to your TikTok account. So you would share your username and password with your assistant so they can assist you with getting things done.

It might also be worth reaching out to influencers who review or share books to see how much it would cost to promote your book and what they would need to make it happen.

Another useful thing is if your assistant has their own TikTok account, they can interact with your videos, answer questions and make sure things are appearing as they should to a normal user. Or they could help manage your second TikTok account that does this too (yes, you should have a silent TikTok account you can watch other things with too).

DISCORD CHANNEL

With Facebook and other platforms limiting what users see unless you pay them, some authors are resorting to other platforms to interact with fans—platforms that allow for ease of interaction without limiting what users see unless the admins want to limit it. Originally intended for gamers and streamers, Discord has taken on new life as a get together spot for many communities, including authors and their fans.

Discord has both text and voice channels. Images can easily be shared on the platform and channels are easily customizable with the ability to add specific sub-channels for whatever you want as an author. You can even have private locked channels for staff to discuss things, channels with rules that only admins can post in, etc. You can share your screen and stream your writing or other work you do if that's something that floats your boat.

Discord is free, but you can boost your channel or your personal account to give bonuses for you or your fans to use or to gain access to additional features.

Unlike Facebook, you can set many levels for access and the

owner of the channel maintains all control, but you can still add admins, moderators and other levels of access as you desire. Even if it is not something you would interact in often, you may still want to have a channel and let the assistant guide things there.

YOUTUBE

YouTube is another way to expand your reach. Whether you are streaming your writing endeavors on Twitch, then porting them to YouTube, reading excepts from your books or sharing other videos you've produced, there are plenty of opportunities to post and share videos on YouTube. You can even put your TikTok videos after you recreate them without the logo on YouTube.

If you do Facebook live videos, you can have your assistant download the videos and upload them to YouTube to create additional content. Note: They have to be an administrator of your Facebook page in order to download the videos.

They can also create some videos on your behalf—like ads and book trailers—if that's something they know how to do. They can then share those on Facebook as well.

If you attend events together, they can film videos of you with fans or working the booth to share on YouTube and other social media platforms as well.

YouTube has a feature where you can add administrators to your account so you do not have to give them your username and password. You can give them full administrative access or limited, depending on what you want them to do. Through this access, they can upload videos, moderate comments, tag videos, create playlists, post on your behalf, and more.

Once you know what you want your assistant to do with YouTube, grant their account the level of access and let them get started.

REDDIT

Reddit is a dangerous time suck, but it can also be turned into a decent promotion tool if it used correctly.

Authors, or their admin, can create a subreddit for the author where new release announcements, Ask Me Anything (AMAs), upcoming events and more can be posted. If you are against Facebook or Twitter and hope to reach more people, Reddit is a perfect opportunity for it.

There are also subreddits where you or your admin can promote your books. It is important, however, to know the rules of those subreddits and how much self-promotion versus commenting on topics is allowed. (Some allow one self-promotion post to ten comments, or any other variety of rules). There are even subreddits for free books, books on sale, and more.

Know what your goal is out of Reddit and if you are planning to spend time there as well as your assistant, or if it will just be your assistant posting to the channel as a moderator. Determine what you want posted and have that discussion with your assistant and find out if it is something they are comfortable with.

Some people may rather not have a Reddit account and that is something to consider. Others may not want to deal with Reddit because it can be a toxic pit some days/weeks.

As is often the case with social media, if you are new to the platform, learn a bit about it before diving in—especially if your assistant is new or unexperienced with it.

OTHER

Social media is constantly changing and new platforms often come and go. Before you decide to branch out to new accounts that your assistant will help out with, be sure to make sure you are not spreading yourself and your assistant too thin. It is easy to think you're doing all the accounts well, but in reality, one or two are being shortchanged in exchange for more being done on the other platforms—this is especially true when ads are involved.

It is always possible to pull back from accounts if you or your assistant are spread too thin. This will allow you/them to focus on the platforms that matter most and then spread to other platforms when it is feasible in the future.

PART TWO

TOOLS FOR SCHEDULING

SCHEDULING POSTS AND SOCIAL MEDIA CALENDAR

One of the most important tasks any assistant can do is to schedule posts for various social media platforms through the platforms themselves (where available) or through a scheduling app.

While many apps cost money to schedule posts to multiple platforms, there are a few that are free if you only have a few social media accounts.

Part of scheduling includes, but is not limited to, figuring out a calendar for posting. The calendar would include preorder postings, release posts, sharing Bookfunnel or StoryOrigin promotions you are signed up for, holiday postings, questions that generate interaction and more.

Knowing how many times per week you wish to post, and any specific posts you want them to make is a good thing to discuss with them. Any additional things you post on one platform and want them to be posted on other platforms also need to be relayed.

You may want posts shared to your groups after they are posted to your Facebook Page. Unfortunately, you can't schedule a post to be shared into a group. You have to share it to the group manually. If you want your assistant to do that, be sure to let them know you want it done.

Do not forget, your assistant can also schedule posts to automatically post within groups as well.

The following sections talk about scheduling posts within the specific platforms, as well as some of the various scheduling applications available and a bit about them.

TOOLS BUILT INTO THE PLATFORMS THEMSELVES

Some social media platforms, such as Facebook, Instagram via your Facebook Page, Pinterest, Patreon and YouTube, can schedule posts from within the platforms themselves, both in their apps and through their websites. It easily allows you and your assistant to see what has been scheduled and posted, anything that has missed posting, and more in a nice calendar or list format.

Depending on how many platforms you are posting to, and if you want to keep your messages similar and save time, you may use the built-in scheduling or a social media scheduling platform to handle scheduling out social media posts.

Once you have your social media calendar figured out, you can have your assistant schedule posts up to a month out. If you have to wait on a release or for a preorder link to be available, they can schedule everything else and come back to schedule those when they're available.

If you are considering a social media scheduling platform, the next section discusses things to consider when choosing that option.

It is good to note here, however, that scheduling posts just takes part of one segment of social media. It does not handle responding to comments on ads or posts, nor does it handle interaction with followers by liking their comments, answering questions and messages to your page, etc. That still has to be handled on a regular, if not daily, basis.

SOCIAL MEDIA SCHEDULING APPS AND WEBSITES

Not long after social media took off, developers and users started looking for ways to schedule posts to automate their engagement and save time. And let's be honest, scheduling posts saves us a lot of time and hassle, especially when you can schedule a few days, weeks, or even a month ahead. This ensures regular activity and thus visibility and reach to your social media accounts.

If you have multiple platforms to post to and want a similar message to be posted and just tweaked (possibly) for the platform, there are many scheduling apps/platforms out there that make it easier to schedule posts for multiple accounts. Most of them allow you to tweak the posts as needed for each platform.

The list below contains just some of the social media scheduling platforms that I am aware of, but more are developed on a regular basis and I'm sure some may disappear or merge with another platform in the future:

- Buffer
- CoSchedule
- eClincher

- Hootsuite
- Later.com
- Loomly
- MavSocial
- PromoRepublic
- Social Pilot
- SproutSocial
- Zoho Schedule

The biggest thing many of these schedulers have in common is the need for a higher paid account level if you do not want to give access to your personal scheduling account in order for your assistant to schedule everything. The next similarity is if you have more than a set number of social media accounts (it varies according to platform), you will have to upgrade to a higher tier or decide if you want to use the platform's scheduling service (if available).

They are also not cheap. The more people or accounts you want to add, the more expensive it gets.

There are things to consider before deciding on a scheduler:

- How many social media platforms do you need to schedule for? Will you be using any of the built-in schedulers to assist?
- What social media platforms will you be using the scheduler for? If you are looking for a platform for TikTok, be sure the scheduler will let you schedule as many as you need for it (or if it will schedule to TikTok at all).
- Does your assistant already have a scheduler and needs to add your accounts to their program? Note: this would require you to give them your username and password for your various accounts, but if you

have them under NDA and trust them, this might save you a cost that they already have for their own business—assuming you do not need them to add a ton of accounts.

- Are you willing to share your account password for the scheduler with your assistant, or do you want to pay for a higher tier and grant them access to your account?
- Who will do the scheduling? Will you be scheduling things alongside them or will they be doing most of the scheduling? (If they are doing most of the scheduling, you may consider just giving them access to your account).

If you give them access to your scheduler account, they can take control of your scheduler account, BUT, if you do not share your individual account passwords, you can deactivate those accounts temporarily in the scheduler by simply changing the passwords. Afterward, you can go through the process to retrieve your account through email. I do strongly recommend setting up two-factor authentication if possible for any scheduler app you use. if your assistant needs a one-time access code, provide it for access. This would also be a good situation to use an app similar to LastPass that would allow you to "share" access to the account without giving them the password and it would allow you to revoke access just as easily without your account becoming compromised.

CREATING CUSTOM GRAPHICS

Building your brand, staying on brand, and keeping with your brand's style with unique graphics is a major part of social media.

Whether you are looking to create special holiday graphics, sales promotion graphics, new release promotion graphics, Facebook/Twitter/Pinterest banners, Facebook ad images, or something else entirely for social media, if your assistant is good with creating graphics, or will learn how to create them (whether with an online app or with a program like Photoshop or Affinity Photo), creating graphics especially for social media can be good use of your assistant's time—especially if they are scheduling social media posts as well.

As mentioned in the previous graphics section, make sure your assistant knows what you want, if you want any special holiday graphics (and for which holidays), promotion graphics etc. Enough ahead of time so that they can do a good job creating what is needed for social media platforms.

DOING TAKEOVERS FOR GROUPS AS AUTHOR PAGE (WHERE POSSIBLE)

As Facebook continues to expand and change, it is becoming easier to join in and take part in group takeovers as your author page.

While not all groups allow pages to join, those that allow the page to take over should allow you to let your admin run the takeover for you. Note: *Not all groups or authors will allow/want your assistant to take over for you. They may want you as the author to do the takeover and that can be understandable, especially if their readers like to connect with you on a personal level, which is what results in book sales.*

If you have examples of previous take overs you've participated in, show your assistant those so they have an idea of normal things you do when you take part.

If you do not have examples, create a living document with posts, answers to common questions, giveaways, trivia and more that they can use as a reference when scheduling posts.

Discuss with them how many posts you want to see scheduled/posted on your behalf and any things you want/do not want them doing. Make sure they are comfortable running takeovers for you as well.

They could also take over other pages on your behalf, scheduling posts, interacting with fans and more without them even knowing you are not behind it.

Ultimately, this is about another way to spread the word about your books and about yourself as an author. If you have a scheduling conflict and cannot do them yourself, or do not have the time to do as many as you would like, having your assistant take them on is not a bad way to go.

SOCIAL MEDIA SWAPS WITH OTHER AUTHORS

Similar to newsletter swaps, authors will sometimes set up social media swaps with similar authors.

These can be set up and scheduled just like newsletter swaps are, but it is a good idea to let your assistant know if you will share only in your group, in your group and page, or other social media options depending on the author you are swapping with. It is also good to know what you want to swap for and how often.

For example, are you just swapping for book ones in a series? Series promotions? Author interviews? Or something else?

And if you change your mind about doing social media swaps, be sure your assistant knows that as well, so they do not schedule some after the fact.

You might even consider putting BookBub follows and recommendations under this if you want to swap BookBub follows/recommendations with a fellow author.

PART ELEVEN

WEBSITE UPDATES

One of the most overwhelming and time-consuming tasks an author has to deal with is their website.

Keeping the content up to date is often just one of many things one must do to keep the website current. Whether an author wants to keep parts of updating the website for themselves, such as regular blog posts, or have an assistant help with it, that's entirely up to you.

Some ideas regarding website tasks an assistant can take over follow. Use those to decide what tasks you wish to free yourself from.

BLOG POSTS

Content, content, content. Whether you are writing content and they post it for you, they are writing content for you, posting a copy of your newsletter to the blog, sharing promotions you participate in, or any number of other things or combination of things above, giving your readers a reason to visit your website is important.

With the way things are changing with email and everything else, your website should be a funnel for sales. And if there is regular new content for readers to enjoy, the more likely they will return to your website of their own free will and higher chances of them purchasing from you.

Talk to your assistant about what you want them to do and what they are comfortable doing as far as content and blog posts are concerned and work from there.

Who knows, you may find an amazing ghost writer for your website as your assistant.

ADDING BOOKS AND OTHER CONTENT

The main point of your website, besides letting people know who you are, is to sell your books. Of course, adding books to the website is a boring and time-consuming job, especially if you rapid release and have a new series regularly.

Having your assistant add your books to whatever system you are using would be a good use of an assistant's time. Once they learn the system, they can easily add in your books with links so your visitors can just click on the link from your website and go directly to wherever they want to purchase the books from.

This is even more important if you have a pen name and multiple sites to maintain with book listings.

It is a win-win.

Be sure to train them on the system if they are not familiar with it or if there are specific things you want done. While some systems are pretty intuitive for adding books to them, others are not. Training shouldn't take a lot of time and is probably something they can easily learn, especially if they are already familiar with the content management system you use.

WEBSITE MAINTENANCE—PLUGINS, BACKUPS, ETC.

Making sure your website stays up to date, whether you are using WordPress, Joomla, or other content management systems, is an important task. Another one—we constantly tell authors to back up their writing in multiple places. The same should apply to your website.

If you use WordPress, there are several free and professional versions of plugins that make excellent backups of your site. Some even do it automatically and do it both on your server and to cloud services, such as OneDrive or Dropbox.

Having your assistant take the time to update your site—especially WordPress—can save you time. Make sure they do backups before a major update. Nothing sucks worse than doing an update and then losing your site. Another reason to do backups—in case your site gets hacked and you need to restore to a version before the hack.

While these tasks do not take a lot of time, they need to be done regularly (especially updating if you have WordPress), and they can add up to a decent amount of time, eventually. If your assistant can do it, it is one less thing for you to do.

SETTING UP AND MANAGING CONTESTS

There are a few plugins and apps that can run contests through your website. Your assistant can handle setting up, creating graphics, writing the copy and promotion for the contest.

Of course, if you do not own one of the apps, they can set them up through the websites for them as well and then create a blog post talking about the contest and link to it. They can handle drawing the winner, contacting them and getting the relevant information needed to send out the prize and either provide it to you to send out the prize or handle it themselves and invoice you for it. They can also announce the winners.

Be sure you know how you want to handle things for each contest and relay that to your assistant along with information such as duration the contest will run, if it is open to U.S. Residents only or to residents of other countries as well, and how prize distribution will occur.

OTHER

There are other tasks your assistant can handle for you on your website, depending on what you want your website to do (or already does).

Do you have e-commerce on your site? Do you have inventory that needs to be added to the site (such as signed books, book crates, various swag for sale, etc.)? Do you have items for sale on another site like Society 6 or Redbubble but want to link to products from your website to show what's available?

Perhaps you have a character database that you want your assistant to work on and maintain. Or a wiki imbedded into your site or on a sub-domain of your site.

Or maybe you're looking for a website redesign or new graphics for the website. If your assistant knows how to do either of those things, it could be a task they take on—especially if they are designing a site on a staging site.

There are many extraneous tasks within website updates you may know about that you can see if your assistant wants to take on.

PART TWELVE

PROOFING

Any author knows, it does not matter how many times you go through your manuscript, errors will slip through. Errors can be reduced by having a proofreader(s) go through the manuscript looking for typos and formatting errors.

But there are several tasks that can fall into the realm of proofreading that your assistant could help with, including audiobook proofing, verifying and compiling changes submitted by your ARC/proofreading team; making changes once verified or even proofreading your novel.

This section goes into detail about those tasks and how they can help you.

AUDIOBOOKS

It is always a good idea to have someone proof your audiobooks. This often involves listening to the audiobook and reading along in the book, noting any errors, including but not limited to names being mispronounced, words being mispronounced, or words or entire paragraphs missing from the manuscript and more. It could even include whether the tone is right for the scene,

Joanna Penn has an article on her website about what to look for when proofing an audio file. You can check it out here: https://www.thecreativepenn.com/2020/11/19/proof-audiobook/

If this is something your assistant will take on to help ensure you have good quality audiobooks, it could be a good assignment for them when the audiobooks become available to proof.

VERIFYING AND UPDATING DRAFT CHANGES BASED ON ARC/PROOFREADER FEEDBACK

It can take a significant chunk of time to review, verify, and then update changes to your manuscript based on feedback provided by your ARC or proofreader team. It can take even longer depending on how you gather their feedback.

If your assistant has a good grasp on grammar and punctuation and will ask you when they have questions about the story that they do not know the answer to, having your assistant take on going through suggested changes and accepting them and making them or ignoring them might be a good task for them to take on.

Obviously, with the first couple of books, you may review their process with them so you can see if they understand what they are doing and why or why not to accept certain suggested changes. It is also a good idea to let them know if you have a reader who likes to suggest a lot of changes that are not right so they can know that going into the process. They should also keep an eye out for any typos or layout issues the team misses and correct those as well.

As always, it does not matter how many people review your manuscript, errors will pop up down the road that will need to be addressed, but at least the majority were caught with your team and assistant.

PROOFREADING A NOVEL TO CHECK FORMATTING AND ANY OTHER ERRORS

If your assistant is not the one who makes the corrections and changes to formatting received from your ARC/proofreader team, it might be a good idea for them to look over the manuscript one last time to check for formatting issues or other errors that were missed by the team.

It never hurts to have another set of eyes review the book before it is published.

PART THIRTEEN

IN-PERSON EVENTS

Helping prior to and during in-person events is an excellent task for an assistant. Whether they live local to you and travel with you to local events, are flown in to events to assist, or set things up ahead of time remotely and let you handle the in-person details will determine what tasks need to be completed.

Making sure swag, paperbacks, business cards, and other materials are ordered and arrive in time for the event are important tasks to be considered well before the event—especially when printing big orders to be shipped somewhere for a signing or sales event.

BOOKING

Many assistants can handle researching and even registering for events on your behalf. They may, depending on the event, be able to commit to the event as well and pay any fees on your behalf, which they would be reimbursed. Other events may require you to sign off on the official contracts and pay for things yourself.

If you want your assistant to keep an eye out for potential signing events for you to sell and sign books, be sure to provide them with pertinent information:

- Any dates you do not want to book events for.
- Max number of days you want run a booth.
- Any events you attended in the past that you do not want to do in the future or any events you attended in the past and would want to attend in the future.
- How much you are willing to spend for a table at events.
- If you want them to pay fees and bill you for them or if you want the bills to come to you for payment.

- Any other important information you think they may need to know.

Communication for booking and planning upcoming events is very important. Making sure they clearly understand what you want and expect from the events they book will help immensely before they get started.

PART ONE

MANAGING THE TABLE

A lot goes into setting up for events the day before or the day of the event opening. There is more to it than just signing up and setting up your table. If your assistant is local to you, they can help with everything from lunch, to setting up the display, selling books and more.

This section will cover many of the potential tasks an assistant could help with at a local event.

TABLE SETUP

Anyone who has set up a table for any type of show knows it takes a significant amount of time to set up the displays and make them look good, as well as packing up the table up once the event is done.

If you have a local assistant, or one that will travel with you to events, they could help set up the table by themselves or with your assistance. Setup will often go a lot faster and smoother with two people moving things in and putting it together. Even though breaking down a table takes a lot less time than setting it up, having them help with that can be useful as well.

It is important to consider that you will pay them for their time at the event and any other costs that may come into play with them being there.

BOXES

There are often a lot of boxes involved when setting up for an event. Those boxes may have books, swag, pens, stuff for give-aways, table decorations and more.

Having an assistant help move boxes into the event center, pull items from them and set up what is in them is a great use of time. They can also store boxes with extra inventory beneath tables or at the back of the booth and then move inventory out when books sell.

Once an event is over, they can consolidate the boxes and move them out to your vehicle for you or help you mail them back home, depending on where you're at and the opportunities available.

LUNCH AND BREAKS

You always need someone at your booth when you need to take a break. Your assistant can make sales for you, monitor the booth and answer questions while you're away. If someone is looking for a signed book, they can get the dedication and their number and then text them when you return so they can get the book(s) signed.

It is important for you to take lunch breaks, bathroom breaks and check out other booths while you are at events. You never know what ideas you might get from seeing other booths or who you might chat with when getting lunch or taking a break.

ASSIST WITH SIGNINGS, ETC.

A lot of work goes into setting up for signings at events. Whether it is at the booth where they are signing for purchasers, or at a special signing event, there are things an assistant can do to ease the pain of such an event.

If it is a specific signing event, they can find out and put the name wanted for the inscription on a sticky note, put the sticky note on the page where the inscription and signature will go and stack the books for the author to be able to easily open to and sign. Then you, or your assistant, can remove the sticky note and hand the book to the fan. They can also have extra pens ready to go for when your pen inevitably stops working in the middle of a signing. This can be done if they are helping you sign books for mailing out to fans as well.

Having an efficient setup for signings makes them run smoothly and go faster, which can be important if you have limited time and many people wanting books.

TAKING PROMO PHOTOS AND SHARING ON SOCIAL MEDIA

Having an assistant take photos of your booth, of you working the booth, of you with fans at the booth, or signing books are great opportunities. Those photos can be shared in your newsletter and on social media.

If you're on TikTok, you can have your assistant film clips from events for your account too.

If you want to get fans to say something for your videos, be sure to get your assistant to get signed releases for them before filming them.

Your assistant could also check out other booths and take pictures of booth setups if you want to find a new way to display your books or brainstorm ideas from the pictures.

ANSWERING QUESTIONS AND HANDLING SALES

Potential new readers, as well as fans, often have a lot of questions about upcoming releases, series, characters and more when they chat with an author. While many authors will answer the questions while at the booth, sometimes it is easier for an assistant to answer some questions while the author is talking to other fans.

They can also help with sales and handing out swag to fans while you handle other things at the event.

PART FOURTEEN

KEEPING YOU ON TRACK

One of the most important things your assistant can do is keep track of things you need to get completed and when you need them completed by. Whether they maintain a calendar you look at, or have things in a list so you can ask them questions and they can answer.

There are many things they can do to help keep you organized and meeting your deadlines.

REMIND YOU OF DEADLINES

Keeping a calendar and reminding you of important deadlines is a simple task for assistants to help you with.

There are many deadlines for an author to meet. And as any author knows all too well, it is easy to forget something, even with calendar reminders scheduled. Having a person prompt you, besides scheduled reminders, is a great way to make sure they are not missed.

MAINTAINING TO-DO LISTS

Every author has to-do lists for themselves and for their assistant to do when a book launches, is on promotion, preparing for an in-person book sale, etc.

Some lists can be easily duplicated when they can be repeated and changed for what's needed. Other lists might be unique depending on what they are for. For example, when I have a lot of books to add to a website and I do them in a batch, I create a to-do list for those updates, which is unique every time I update the website. How detailed or general those lists are are up to you and your assistant.

There are also many great programs you can use to help track your to-do lists. What you use is up to you. I often use a combination of Google Keep, Trello, and a written planner to keep track of my current tasks and upcoming tasks.

Below is a list of platforms you can use to help you and your author to track task for projects. This list is not complete, but are the ones I know of or have had recommended to me in the past. What you two decide to use should be based on comfort levels using the platforms.

1. Trello
2. Asana
3. Airtable
4. Monday.com
5. Workzone
6. Smartsheet
7. Jira
8. Google Keep
9. Google spreadsheets
10. ClickUp

PART FIFTEEN

MISCELLANEOUS

There are some tasks that do not fall into the chapters above that an assistant can help with. These are just a few of those tasks, but there are many others. If there is something you want your assistant to take care of, discuss it with them and see if it is something they'd be willing to take on.

For example, I know of one assistant who not only helps with graphics, social media scheduling, promotion and website maintenance, she also does meal planning and grocery list creation for her clients because it is one less thing for them to have to think and worry about.

SETTING UP (IF NOT SET UP) AND MAINTAINING MERCHANDISE SHOP

Merchandising is an important part of additional income you can gain while being an author, but it can also be time-consuming. Finding the right site based on what products you want to offer, setting up the artwork, adding new artwork and making sure you have the right licensing for artwork before you sell the products all add up.

If you have not already decided on a site, your assistant can check out various options, let you know what percentage you would make off of sales, what products they have—especially if they have specific products you want to have produced, and any quality issues as seen in reviews can make it easier for you to decide which site to use.

Once decided, they can take care of getting the artwork set up for each product design, provide you with proofs and let the shop go from there.

If you have custom products on hand to sell, you could ship them to your assistant and have them ship them out for you (and of course be reimbursed for shipping).

DESIGNING AND ORDERING PROMOTIONAL MATERIALS FOR EVENTS (SWAG, BANNERS, POSTERS, ETC.)

A wide variety of promotional products can be designed and ordered for in-person events and for sending to super fans.

Bookplates are often an item authors forget to have designed or printed for events. These allow for them to sign stickers that fans can then put inside the book of their choice if they do not bring or buy books at the event for the author to sign. They're also great to sign and ship to fans.

Some authors print postcards with the cover of their books on them to sign for fans.

Then there's a variety of swag, including but not limited to:

- Bookmarks
- Bracelets
- Business cards
- Buttons
- Candy
- Pens
- Pop sockets
- Stickers

- Themed boxes

The first thing you and your assistant will need to decide is which vendor(s) you will use for your products. If you know of an author who has had specific swag at events that you liked, you might reach out to them for their recommendations. Or you may ask in various Facebook groups. Rarely will one vendor be able to create everything you want for swag. Some come close, but I have found I can get better deals when I work with companies who specialize in certain products (for example, pop sockets and buttons). This will allow you to determine what graphics will need to be created to order proofs and products.

Allowing your assistant to create proofs of the products you want, reviewing them, and letting them order quantities requested on your behalf can save a lot of time and worry out of taking care of this task.

Discuss with your assistant whether you want them to use your business debit or credit card or PayPal account to purchase the items, or if they should purchase the items with their own accounts and be reimbursed by you.

Alternatively, they can set everything up for you and have you go in and pay for everything.

SERIES BIBLE

If it looks like your series could turn into a world/universe with lots of series and/or you are planning to allow other authors to write in your world, creating a world bible for them, as well as yourself, is essential.

If you have not created one from the very beginning and want to, your assistant could take on that task to build the initial version of it, then you could go in behind them and update/correct it as needed. If you *have* created one, but it is running behind due to new books being written and the document not updated, or because other authors have written in the shared world but their additions have not been added, your assistant could take on that task.

This does, of course, require them reading the books and being very detail-oriented with creating or updating a series bible. This also means it will be time-consuming and it may cause questions as well—or potentially finding errors that need to be corrected.

This begs the question, are you paying them to read your books? Technically, yes and technically no. If they are reading or re-reading them to build your series bible, you are really paying the to build the bible. But reading and rereading is required to get the details correct because we all have faulty memories.

One topic to discuss is how detail oriented you are expecting the bible to be and if there are specific things you need in it. For example, family trees, eye/hair color, relationships, etc.

As with some of the other tasks, it is probably a good idea for you to review the Series Bible and make sure what they are providing is correct and advise them of changes you would like as well as what you like about what they are doing to help keep things moving smoothly.

WIKIS FOR FANS

Whether you run a wiki on your own website or host it through Fandom or one of the other wiki sites, having a wiki where fans can contribute information and your assistant makes sure information is accurate/correct the information can come in handy.

Your assistant can also help populate the wiki with content. If they have not read the books yet, or even if they have, it will take re-reading them.

If you plan to have a reading order for books in the series or family trees for characters, the wiki would be a good place for those which would then allow you to link to the character profiles.

This could also be useful in creating the series bible mentioned above—you could have a private wiki that only certain people have access to that contains additional information about the world you and others will write in.

Make sure you and your assistant discuss how you want to handle potential spoilers that may appear in the wiki and whether you want a complete plotline summary or just a vague description of the books to prevent the stories from being spoiled and making people not read them since they know what's going on.

COMMUNICATE WITH OTHER TEAM MEMBERS, FELLOW AUTHORS, VENDORS, ETC.

Communication is a very important part of an assistant's job tasks. Not only do they need to communicate with you, but they also need to handle communication for many tasks, including but not limited to:

- Discussing newsletter swaps with authors
- If you work with a publisher, they can turn over manuscripts, discussing deadlines, changes, etc.
- If you have others on your team that handle advertising, they can work with them to help keep those tasks running smoothly
- Working with fans on special projects

No matter what situations pops up, your assistant needs to communicate with everyone professionally.

KEEP AN EYE OUT FOR ANTHOLOGIES TO PARTICIPATE IN

A great way to get your name out there and get more eyes on your writing is to participate in anthologies. While you may hear of some on your own, having your assistant keep an eye out for other anthologies and letting you know when one comes up they think would be a good fit for you to write in is invaluable.

They can provide you with all the information to take part and let you work from there. Then they can remind you of the deadlines as well.

Or, if information is not easily available, they can reach out to the organizer and find out what they need from you and when. Then, when the rights to the story revert to you after the anthology's run is concluded, you have an extra reader magnet to use in the future.

BRAINSTORMING

It is often good to have another person to bounce ideas off of—especially when you discover a plot hole, get stuck writing, or are looking for a way to word something and it just is not coming to you.

Other times, it can be good to just talk through a plot line, character ideas or more. You never know, you may find your assistant has a lot of great ideas that can be useful to your writing as well.

RESEARCH

The devil is in the details, or so they say. Every writer knows what it is like to get lost in a research hole and end up finding out how long it takes a steamboat to go from a port in Germany to London in the 1800s. No? Just me? But you know what I mean. When writing, there are often things you need to research or make notes to research for accuracy. Depending on what you need researched, your assistant could help and do the research for you.

If it is not writing related research, they could do other research as well. Find vendors for various swag or other products, compare vendors for other projects, and more.

If your assistant is good at researching, you may ask them to do other tasks as well where research can be an excellent tool (finding comparison authors, new indie authors, and more).

QUESTIONS TO ASK YOURSELF

Before you look for an assistant(s), there are several questions you should ask yourself.

I suggest you think about your answers for a day or two and write out your answers so you know what you're looking for when you search for an assistant(s).

Questions include:

- What trust are you willing to place in an assistant?
- What is your time worth to you?
- What is their experience, or lack thereof, worth to you?
- Are you willing to train your assistant in tasks they may not know how to do, but will take on? If so, what are some things you would be willing to teach them?
- Are you willing to invest in certain products or programs to make your author career easier?
- What genre(s) are you looking for an assistant to assist with?

- Are you considering one or more assistants?
- What tasks are you willing to give up to another person?
- What tasks are you absolutely unwilling to part with? Why?
- What three tasks are the things that take up most of your time AND you will get rid of?
- What are five tasks after those first three that you do not enjoy doing and want to get rid of?
- Do you prefer to pay a flat rate for the assistant or are you willing for them to track time and bill hourly?
- How often will you pay them? Weekly? Biweekly? Twice monthly? Monthly?
- How will you pay them? PayPal? Zelle? Direct Deposit? Some other way?
- How will you track how much they are paid to send them a 1099?
- Will you be requiring an NDA to be signed? Do you have one already created?
- If they create a contract, are you willing to sign a contract? Or vice versa, will you be creating a contract for them to sign?

Some of these questions may not seem important at first, but as you go through them, you should begin to understand why they are.

WHAT TRUST ARE YOU WILLING TO PLACE IN AN ASSISTANT?

Before you decide what tasks you will have your assistant take on, decide how much trust you will put in them, as that will ultimately determine what tasks you want them to focus on. You may start them with tasks that require relatively low levels of trust so that they can build trust to take on other tasks, or you may trust them from the get go based on recommendations from other clients or other people they have worked with in the past. All of this is based on your comfort level with them, especially if you are sharing passwords or other sensitive information.

I strongly suggest having a signed NDA with your assistant before work begins, as well as any other necessary paperwork done. While strictly speaking, the NDA does not prevent them from betraying trust and doing things against your best interest, it is a legal document that can carry some weight in court if things go downhill.

WHAT IS YOUR TIME WORTH TO YOU?

This is one of the most important questions to consider. If you could put a monetary value on what your time is worth to you, what would it be? Are you willing to pay that amount to an assistant to free up your time so you can write more or do other tasks only you can do?

Are you willing to pay an experienced assistant that amount if they require little to no training to take on tasks? Are you willing to pay someone less, knowing you will train them to take on tasks you want done because it will be worth it in the long run (even if they use those skills to help other authors in the future)?

It is also a good idea to give your assistant raises as they get better at what they do. I suggest evaluating your assistant after 90 days and give them a raise, then another at 6 months, then up to you after that. If you have a person who turns out to be an excellent assistant and helping you out at their tasks, they will be worth what you are paying them, possibly more.

Unfortunately, I have seen some authors who believe virtual assistants should work for very little or free. I will be the first person to tell them they are wrong. People should be paid for the work they do. It does not matter that they are working for you virtually, they are working for you and taking things off your plate. They deserve to be paid for their time.

I also believe if your spouse or child are working for you, they should be paid as well—especially if your author career is moving to the next level. Paying them, even if they are family, can help come tax time.

WHAT IS THEIR EXPERIENCE, OR LACK THEREOF, WORTH TO YOU?

This question goes hand-in-hand with the previous question.

Assistants come with various levels of experience. Some are authors who are looking to make extra money until their career as an author gets off the ground. Some are people who are dipping their feet into the field of assistant work for authors because they hear it is a way to make decent money and have very little experience. Others have experience in fields that could come in handy for being an author's assistant even if they have never been one before (for example, project managers, administrative assistants, office assistants, journalists, any job that requires multitasking, etc.)

Assistants who have been doing this for years and have a client list who is extremely happy with them may be higher priced and may not have the availability to take on new clients. Or they may only have the capacity to take on certain tasks for new clients.

Others who specialize in Facebook, Amazon, and/or BookBub ads and are known for their successes may be only interested in taking on clients who make over a certain income with their books and have a significant backlist.

Assistants that are new to the job or have some experience but still need some training will cost less but may take more time investment to get them up to speed.

Understandably, long-time established assistants will have a higher price to start than an assistant who is not established or is newly established. Long-time established assistants are often in high demand and their rates are based on the demand and the work they do for authors and how happy their clients have been with their works. This does not mean that other assistants will not do as good as a job, it just means they are still learning and getting good at what they are doing and in order to build their business, they are charging less.

When you look into assistants, I would suggest not looking at paying anyone less than $20-30 an hour for their work and know what the max is that you will pay based on what tasks you want them to do. Then know what you would be willing to pay someone with little to no experience versus someone with a lot of experience. For example, you may pay someone who does advertising more per hour than someone who is handling day-to-day tasks that do not include advertising. I also advise paying your child or spouse if they do assistant work for you. It is work and they are helping to grow your author business.

ARE YOU WILLING TO TRAIN YOUR ASSISTANT IN TASKS THEY MAY NOT KNOW HOW TO DO, BUT WILL TAKE ON? IF SO, WHAT ARE SOME THINGS YOU WOULD BE WILLING TO TEACH THEM?

If you bring on a new or relatively new assistant who has little experience, you may need to train them how to do certain tasks. Even if you have a more experienced assistant, if you want things done a certain way (perhaps you want them to know how you choose your categories or you want them to do manuscript changes a certain way), show them how you do it.

If you know there are certain tasks you want done a certain way that you would have to train any assistant on, I would suggest creating a written and/or video guide for specific tasks. This would be something that would be evergreen and can be reused if you change assistants in the future or bring on additional people to do other tasks. If you have to train them on something else, it does not hurt to create a guide for that because you never know if you'll have to train someone else to do that in the future as well.

ARE YOU WILLING TO INVEST IN CERTAIN PRODUCTS OR PROGRAMS TO MAKE YOUR AUTHOR CAREER EASIER?

While many assistants will already own many programs that are useful to being an author's assistant (for example, PublisherRocket, KDP Spy, etc.), there may be other programs they do not have, but that you want them to use.

Some programs, like social media scheduling apps or task managers, can be bought and paid for by you and then assigned to them to use. If there are programs you want them to use that would be useful for other clients, you could buy it for them, but it is probably wiser to encourage them to save up money and purchase it themselves and then use it as a tax write-off instead of purchasing it for them.

If you have specific fonts you want used that are paid fonts, despite them being able to keep it afterward as there is no way to force them to give up the font(s), I would suggest buying them the license for the fonts. That way everything is on the up-and-up and you have the correct licensing work for anything they create on your behalf.

WHAT GENRE(S) ARE YOU LOOKING FOR A ASSISTANT TO ASSIST WITH?

You may be thinking 'this is not a question I need to ask myself', but for some authors, it is.

Some authors have a pen name or two (or three) that write in different genres. And sometimes you want to keep those personas different, which may mean having a different assistant for each pen name or having an assistant who is comfortable and familiar with working with different genres.

For example, you may write cozy mysteries under your real name, but paranormal romance under a pen name and space opera under a different pen name. You obviously want an assistant who would know the genres well and while some have some crossover, other genres do not.

So knowing which genre(s) you want your assistant to assist with is an important thing to know before you look for one.

WHAT TASKS ARE YOU WILLING TO GIVE UP TO ANOTHER PERSON? WHY?

Having a list of tasks you would like to not have to do regularly can help you determine if you need one or more assistants. Keep in mind, the 'why' could be as simple as "I hate doing this task" or "this task takes up too much of my time and I need to spend that time writing or working on other tasks."

This list makes shopping for an assistant easier as well. You can provide the list to a potential assistant and they can tell you if they know how to do them, which ones they can't, or will not, do and which ones they may need training on.

Ultimately, it makes it easier for you and them if you go into your search knowing what tasks you do not want to do anymore. Far too often, many authors do not know what they want their assistant to do, what they *can* do, and what they *will* do... and then expect the assistant to just read their minds. Go back through the lists in this book and decide on a personalized list of potential tasks an assistant could take on.

WHAT TASKS ARE YOU ABSOLUTELY UNWILLING TO PART WITH? WHY?

Much like the previous task, knowing what tasks you are unwilling to allow someone else to do (and why you are unwilling to let them take it on) is invaluable.

For example, you may not want your assistant to handle uploading books and doing corrections for you because it would mean they have access to your KDP and Amazon accounts, and you do not want to put your account at risk. Or it could be you do not want to ask them to do certain tasks, like uploading to publishers via Direct2Digital, until you know them well enough and it looks like things are working out well with them as an assistant.

Of course, there may be some tasks you do not want them to do at all because you are comfortable doing them yourself, and that is perfectly fine.

WHAT THREE TASKS ARE THE THINGS THAT TAKE UP MOST OF YOUR TIME AND YOU CAN GET RID OF?

Once you have figured out what tasks you want to get rid of and which ones you want to keep doing yourself, I suggest figuring out the first three tasks you want your assistant to take on.

In an informal poll of authors who have assistants and those who do not, the overwhelming majority said these they would give up these things:

1. Social media management
2. Newsletter swaps (and newsletter writing and management)
3. (Tied) Proofreading OR on-going promotions (booking promotion sites, etc.) OR AMS keyword curation and maintenance

Social media management, by far, beat out everything below it. It comes as no surprise that social media management topped the list. It is a time suck. When you think you will only spend 15 or 20 minutes working on it, the next thing you know, you've wasted hours of time that you could have spent writing. Then you spend time writing, and your social media presence dwindles!

With all the changes to social media platforms, it really helps to have someone who reacts, likes and responds to comments on your page(s) and ads. If they can schedule posts as well, then you have far fewer things to take up time.

After you create your top 3 list, I suggest adding more to it until you have a top 5 and a top 10 list (or top whatever number) of tasks you would like an assistant to take on. That way you know what other tasks you want them to do when they have the capacity and ability to do so.

ARE YOU CONSIDERING ONE OR MORE ASSISTANTS?

If you are looking for only one assistant, knowing what tasks you want them to take on will help you narrow down your search. If you are looking for one to help with day-to-day tasks and one to assist with advertising, then you know what specialized assistants you need to look for. Or, if you're looking for one for each of your pen names (if you have more than one), then you know what genre(s) you need them to specialize in.

DO YOU PREFER TO PAY A FLAT RATE FOR AN ASSISTANT OR ARE YOU WILLING FOR THEM TO TRACK TIME AND BILL HOURLY?

How you pay your assistant and how your assistant wants to get paid is an important point to discuss before any agreement for work is reached. Some assistants have a flat rate that they charge for accomplishing certain predetermined tasks each week. They may break this down by telling you what they will do each week for each pay tier. Others will do as much work as you want them to do at an hourly rate.

There is no wrong way to go about this, but knowing how they want to do it allows you to plan things out.

You may also want to discuss how many hours a week you want them to dedicate to helping you each week. If you are only expecting them having 5-10 hours of work a week, then they could take on other clients and not be a detriment to the tasks you want them to do. If you want them for closer to 20 or 30 hours, then they'd need to know if they can take you on as a client.

Most assistants who offer flat rates for set tasks done each week have established those tasks and how long it takes for them to accomplish them because they know they can take on other clients and get the same type of work done in the same time and they do not have to worry about running out of capacity if they do not overbook themselves.

HOW OFTEN WILL YOU PAY THEM? WEEKLY? BIWEEKLY? TWICE MONTHLY? MONTHLY?

Payroll. For any business owner, payroll is an important part of the business—even if the person in question is a contractor.

You will want to discuss with your assistant how often you are going to pay them. They may want to be paid every week, or every two weeks, or whenever works for you. Knowing when they are going to be paid for work done can ease worry with finances for you and them. It is good to note some authors prefer their assistant invoice them at the end of the month so they can pay at the beginning of the next month because it coincides with when they get paid by Amazon and other publishing sites.

Make sure your assistant knows when you want to be invoiced if they are flexible with when they are being paid. Also establish when and how you are going to pay them. If you are in the U.S., be sure to get a W-9 from them so you can file the paperwork when tax season comes due. If you are in other countries, research what tax paperwork and responsibilities you have when you pay an independent contractor for work.

HOW WILL YOU PAY THEM? PAYPAL? ZELLE? DIRECT DEPOSIT? SOME OTHER WAY?

Knowing how your assistant would prefer to be paid, and what you have available to pay them, is good to know ahead of time.

There are many ways to pay someone these days—it just depends on what service your assistant has or will join in order to get paid. If you are set up with Direct Deposit, paying them this way is safe and secure, even if it costs a fee each time you use it. Otherwise, there are many options to pay someone no matter where they are in the world. Of course, you can also just write them a check and mail it to them if they do not have a way to receive funds online.

I would suggest you discuss this with them before bringing them on as your assistant. That way, if there is a service they need to be paid by and you can't use it for whatever reason, you do not discover this after they've done work for you and need to be paid.

HOW WILL YOU TRACK HOW MUCH THEY ARE PAID TO SEND THEM A 1099?

For anyone who hasn't had a contract employee(s) before, this is a step that might be overlooked. Make sure you have a way to track how much you pay them, then be sure not only to send them the 1099 they need at the beginning of the following year, but also be sure to file the paperwork with the IRS as an employer as well.

There may be other paperwork you need to file for paying someone who resides in another country or if you are located outside of the U.S. and paying a U.S. employee. Be sure to consult with an accountant in your region to make sure the right paperwork is filed by your country's deadlines.

WILL YOU REQUIRE AN NDA TO BE SIGNED? HAVE YOU ALREADY CREATED ONE?

If you plan to have an assistant(s), it may be a good idea to have them sign a standard non-disclosure agreement (NDA) with you. An NDA helps protect your intellectual property, your marketing plans, and anything else that is specific to your author business.

If you do not have one already created, there are many avenues to go to create one. Talking to a lawyer to get a standard one that you can use for anyone you bring on your team might be a great option, even if it costs a bit. At least you know everything is right for the legal side of things.

Be sure to keep a digital copy of NDAs in multiple places. That way in case something happens and you need to use them in a court case, you have them. Chances are, you will not need them, but it is wise to back up in multiple places.

IF THEY CREATE A CONTRACT, ARE YOU WILLING TO SIGN A CONTRACT? ALTERNATIVELY, WILL YOU BE CREATING A CONTRACT FOR THEM TO SIGN?

Like any business endeavor as an author, whether it is editing or cover design or something else, established assistants may have a contract that they sign with potential clients to ensure when they get paid, their pay rates, etc.

I would never recommend signing a contract blindly. I would, however, suggest reading them and paying close attention to detail and if there are any parts you disagree with, discussing it with them to have it changed or having a lawyer review it in order for suggested changes to be made.

Contracts, much like an NDA, can protect you and them in the long run.

QUESTIONS TO ASK YOUR POTENTIAL ASSISTANT

Many authors I have consulted with do not know what questions to ask when looking for and vetting a potential assistant. Others are not sure if they're asking the right questions to find the right assistant.

That's where I hope these questions will help you out.

Much like the previous chapter, I will explain why these questions are important, but I will also discuss some answers to look out for. But before I go into that, I need to clarify a few things.

Many of the questions are questions you would ask a seasoned assistant. Some would not apply to a virtual assistant just launching their business and trying to gain experience. Had people not taken a risk with me first when I did work as a volunteer to help authors out, then on a paid endeavor, I would not be fortunate enough to be where I am today. I definitely would not be writing this guide for authors.

Those questions, however, are still important to ask a new and upcoming assistant. It will allow you to gauge where they are at and if you will take them on and train them in what they do not know.

Questions to ask a potential assistant include:

- What experience level do you have as a assistant?
- If their experience level is new, or relatively new, do they have a resume that would show skills applicable to assistant work? Do they have a cover letter that states why they think they'd be a good virtual assistant?
- Do you have any references?
- Are you able to multi-task and switch between tasks with ease?
- How good are your time management skills? How about project management?
- Have you ever fired a client? Why?
- Has a client has ever fired you? Why?
- What genres do you have experience with?
- What genres do you not work with?
- What tasks are you willing to take on?
- What are some tasks you would not be willing to take on at all?
- Do you have any of the following programs?
- Publisher Rocket
- KDP Spy
- Scrivener
- Word (or some other word processing program)
- Graphic design programs (GIMP, Photoshop, Illustrator, etc.)
- Vellum, Atticus or other layout programs
- Any specialized programs or apps that you need for your business

- How many hours per week/month are you capable of taking on?
- Are you willing to learn new tasks on your own or with training from the author?
- Are you willing to read books I recommend or research certain tasks to learn how to do them on your own?
- Are you willing to take courses I've paid for? Are you willing to pay for courses for yourself since they would be usable for your other clients as well?
- Do you charge a flat rate or hourly?
- Do you have experience booking promotion sites for [your specific genre]?
- Do you have experience creating custom graphics?
- Tell me about your website updating experience?
- Do you have experience proofing audiobooks?
- Do you have any ARC Team management experience?
- Do you have any experience with other tasks you would like to tell me about?

Each of these questions will follow with explanations as to why I suggest asking them, answers to look for, or answers that should alarm you (if pertinent to the question).

WHAT EXPERIENCE LEVEL DO YOU HAVE AS AN ASSISTANT?

This question is important because it will give you an idea how much or how little training they need. Ask them about their experience in specific tasks that you know you want them to take on as well as ones you may assign in the future.

Ask them to tell you a bit about their work completed for other clients and ask them if they have any examples you can see. Also ask to see their website and/or Facebook page, so you can get an idea about them personally as well. They may have information on their website about the tasks they do and their costs.

IF THEIR EXPERIENCE LEVEL IS NEW, OR RELATIVELY NEW, DO THEY HAVE A RESUME THAT WOULD SHOW SKILLS APPLICABLE TO ASSISTANT WORK? DO THEY HAVE A COVER LETTER THAT STATES WHY THEY THINK THEY'D BE A GOOD VIRTUAL ASSISTANT?

There are many individuals who are interested in breaking into being an assistant, or have just started out and have little to no experience in the work.

Some are authors who need a little more income while releasing books. They may have experience doing several things for themselves and they could tell you about the work they do. Or someone could have been an administrative assistant or project manager (or other job positions—there are too many to list), that would come in handy when being an author's assistant.

Asking to see their resume and cover letter is a great starting point. Interviewing them, besides asking the questions below, for the position is another great way to gauge their experience.

Questions to consider for the interview:

- What makes you think you would be a good assistant?
- What skills do you have that align with assistant work?
- What are your strengths? Weaknesses?
- What task do you think you are good at?

- How do you feel about working with little to no supervision?
- Are you good at prioritizing tasks and meeting deadlines?
- How good are you with being interrupted while doing one task to do another one and going back to the first?
- Think of a potential situation that you have dealt with or know of other authors or their assistants dealing with. Ask them to describe how they would handle the situation.

DO YOU HAVE ANY REFERENCES?

New assistants may not have any references, or may have a few for work they've done as a volunteer.

Established assistants should have several references.

Ask them if it is okay for you to reach out to their past/current clients and get their recommendations from them. Ask for contact information as well.

ARE YOU ABLE TO MULTI-TASK AND SWITCH BETWEEN TASKS WITH EASE?

Multi-tasking is an important part of any assistant's day—especially if they work for multiple clients. Even if they do not work for multiple clients, sometimes interruptions happen and you have to switch concentration from one task to another more important one, then return to the one you were working on.

People do not realize how often tasks can change in a day. Sometimes you can focus on one task for a set amount of time, then switch to a new task. Being able to keep track of the tasks needing to be done and then completing them is part of the multi-tasking required of an author assistant.

Discussing with them how they plan to handle interruptions and multitasking would be a good follow up question to this one. You could even give them an example and see how they respond to it.

HOW GOOD ARE YOUR TIME MANAGEMENT SKILLS? HOW ABOUT PROJECT MANAGEMENT?

These questions go hand-in-hand. Being able to manage their time, projects, and due dates for you and other clients is important. Someone might say they are good at these things, but it is hard to actually tell.

You might ask them how they plan to track tasks they have to do for you and how will they make sure tasks that need to be completed by a due date will be done.

Another option is to ask them to tell you about any experience they have where their time management and project management skills played a role.

HAVE YOU EVER FIRED A CLIENT? WHY?

There are often good reasons an assistant might fire a client. Whether it be lack of payment, lack of communication, lack of time, or not able to expand to keep up with client's demands, find out what it was.

Why? It prevents you from making the same mistake and it lets you know they value their time and are not afraid to put down boundaries.

HAVE YOU EVER BEEN FIRED BY A CLIENT? WHY?

This question is almost as important, if not more so, than the previous question.

Knowing if a client and has ever fired them and the reason will allow you to determine if it is worth giving them a first chance with you. Sometimes, life circumstances get in the way or there is a conflict of personalities with another client that results in being let go. It could also be they were still learning and made too many mistakes. Whatever the reason, it is an important consideration when hiring a new person.

WHAT GENRES DO YOU HAVE EXPERIENCE WITH?

Familiarity with specific genres can play an important role with an assistant—especially when booking promotion sites, researching keywords and comparable authors, etc. While an assistant can learn those necessary genres, you need to know if they are familiar with your genre(s) before you hire them. Some genres and subgenres are close to each other, so if they know the main genre, but not the subgenre, it would not be difficult for them to learn that as well.

You may also ask if they are interested in and willing to learn genres, especially if you write in several and want them to help with other genres, eventually. If they are not familiar with the genres you work with, are you willing to train them in what they need to know to perform the tasks you want them to do for you?

WHAT GENRES DO YOU NOT WORK WITH?

Some people may have very strict genres they will never work with. For example, some may not want to work with erotica or romance with sex on the page. Others may not have an interest in learning about how to market historical fiction or non-fiction.

Knowing what genres are not for them can help you decide if they'll be a match for you.

WHAT TASKS ARE YOU WILLING TO TAKE ON?

This question is important because there may be certain tasks an assistant will take on or learn.

If you hire one that just does Facebook ads or AMS ads, they may not be willing to take on the additional task of the one they do not do. They may also not be interested in taking on Bookbub Ads or other tasks.

Knowing exactly what tasks they already know how to do and want to take on will determine if they are a good fit for the tasks you want to give up.

WHAT ARE SOME TASKS YOU WOULD NOT BE WILLING TO TAKE ON AT ALL

Similar to the previous question, knowing what tasks they would not be willing to take on will help you in deciding.

Not everyone is good at creating graphics, writing blurbs, running ads, or updating websites, or it may just be tasks they do not want to do. Finding out what tasks they are unwilling to take on will let you know if you need to look into hiring more than one assistant to help with other tasks or if you need to find one that will do more of the tasks you want to get rid of.

DO YOU HAVE ANY OF THE FOLLOWING PROGRAMS? HOW FAMILIAR ARE YOU WITH THEM?

- Publisher Rocket
- KDP Spy
- Scrivener
- Word/comparable
- Graphic design programs (GIMP, Photoshop, Illustrator, etc.)
- Vellum, Atticus or other layout programs
- Other programs you think would help with assistant tasks
- Dropbox/OneDrive

Knowing what programs they already own will let you know if they could potentially help you with certain tasks. For example, Publisher Rocket is great for researching categories, keywords and ad keywords—a task an assistant can easily take on for a new series. Vellum/Atticus or other programs and knowing how to use them to format books can be a huge timesaver for you as well.

If there is a program you want them to use for tasks, are you willing to help them purchase it or suggest to them they need to purchase it for future tasks and it is a potential tax write off for their business?

Some assistants may be very willing to learn how to use programs they do not own yet and may not afford some of them until down the road. If they say they will purchase it when they have more flexible funds, you may choose to help them out and buy it for them to help them build their business or wait for them to purchase it before assigning tasks using those programs to them.

HOW MANY HOURS A WEEK/MONTH ARE YOU CAPABLE OF TAKING ON?

Knowing how many hours of work you anticipate an assistant taking on and asking them how much time they have available will help you determine if you need to hire more than one person or just one for the tasks you want to give to your assistant.

There will be some assistants who are doing this in addition to a full- or part-time job to make ends meet. Others will be authors who need income regularly while waiting for their author career to take off and may take up to 20 hours a week. Some may have several clients and are only looking for a few more hours each week or month to get them to however many hours a week they are looking for.

Keep in mind, some tasks may take more or less time than you expect, especially if there are tasks you want them to do that you do not know how to do. Many assistants will be flexible with how many hours a week they can work, but some may not.

Knowing what hours they have available will allow you to determine what tasks they can start with, then see how much time they have available after a week or two before you add more.

ARE YOU WILLING TO LEARN NEW TASKS ON YOUR OWN OR WITH TRAINING FROM THE AUTHOR?

Chances are, especially if the assistant you are hiring is new to working for authors, they will learn how to do new tasks from you. Few new assistants will refuse to learn new things to help build their business.

Experienced assistants might not be as interested in learning new things, especially if they are specialized in assisting in a few tasks, but it does not hurt to ask either.

ARE YOU WILLING TO READ BOOKS I RECOMMEND OR RESEARCH CERTAIN TASKS TO LEARN HOW TO DO THEM ON YOUR OWN?

Most times, they may have already read the books, or own the books that you want them to read to get an idea of certain tasks. If there are specific books, you want them to read that they do not have, buy them copies for them to read if they are not available in KU (if they do not want to buy them for themselves).

Before asking them if they have read any particular book, make sure you have a list of books you want them to read.

ARE YOU WILLING TO TAKE COURSES I HAVE PAID FOR? ARE YOU WILLING TO PAY FOR COURSES FOR YOURSELF SINCE THEY WOULD BE USABLE FOR YOUR OTHER CLIENTS?

There are many valuable courses out there for authors that would be useful for an assistant to go through, whether they intend to be an author themselves. I am reluctant to advertise any in particular, but if there are some you have gone through and think would be useful for your assistant to take, you might see if they would be interested in taking them. Courses can offer a lot of additional insight with ads, keywords, and more.

This question and the past couple of questions should not be questions that determine whether the assistant is a good fit for you, but one to let you know if they are interested in expanding their horizons and learning as they go.

DO YOU CHARGE A FLAT RATE OR HOURLY?

This question is pretty self-explanatory. Some assistants offer a rate to do X many tasks—such as 20 social media posts a week, per month—for a fixed amount. Same with booking newsletter promotional sites. Other assistants may charge hourly rates, especially if they do a variety of tasks for their clients.

Knowing how they charge is a good way to start. Then you can find out how often they want to be paid, and whether they want to be paid before or after work is done.

DO YOU HAVE EXPERIENCE BOOKING PROMOTION SITES FOR [YOUR SPECIFIC GENRE]?

If you are interested in having your assistant handle booking promotion sites for your books when they are on promotion, this is a great question to ask.

While many genres can be submitted to the same sites, some genres, specifically romance and clean romance, have more sites that are targeted just for those genres.

Experience is not strictly necessary, but it can be useful if they know the sites already. If they do not, you may prepare a list of sites you use regularly and any you want to test while they book promotions.

DO YOU HAVE EXPERIENCE CREATING CUSTOM GRAPHICS? DO YOU HAVE ANY EXAMPLES?

If they already have experience creating graphics with Photoshop, Paintshop, Affinity Photo or another program, they would be happy to tell you about it and show examples.

If they do not, and you want them to learn, there are plenty of tutorials on YouTube to teach them how to create simple graphics for promotion, but it may take them longer to do it. Creating with BookBrush or something else might be a more efficient use of their time.

TELL ME ABOUT YOUR WEBSITE UPDATING EXPERIENCE?

This is a great opportunity to learn what, if any experience, an assistant has at updating websites. You will want to know if they are familiar with WordPress or other CMS platforms, or will learn them.

You might ask them exactly what experience they have and what they are comfortable doing. If they do not have experience with your website CMS, you may need to train them if they are interested.

DO YOU HAVE EXPERIENCE PROOFING AUDIOBOOKS?

If they have experience, ask them what the experience is and whose audiobooks they have proofed before. If not, tell them what you are looking for when proofing audiobooks and see if they are interested in adding that to their task list.

DO YOU HAVE ANY ARC TEAM MANAGEMENT EXPERIENCE?

Do you have any ARC Team management experience?

Running an ARC Team can be a challenge. It takes some time to get them to run efficiently and if someone already has experience, it is worth seeing how they have run ARC teams before and if they enjoyed it or not.

You might ask them who they have run ARC Teams for, and an example of how they ran the group.

If they do not have any experience, you might ask them how they would run an ARC team on your behalf. If their process differs from yours, you might discuss it with them and see if you can find a compromise on how to run your ARC team if you want them to take it on.

DO YOU HAVE ANY EXPERIENCE WITH OTHER TASKS YOU WOULD LIKE TO TELL ME ABOUT?

There are many tasks from other jobs that can carry over as experience for assistants. That experience could even include being an author themselves and doing certain tasks for themselves. Or it could be a day job where they are required to multi-task and manage multiple projects.

It is always good to see what other experiences a potential employee has because you never know how it is useful to you in the future.

IMPORTANT THINGS TO
REMEMBER

COMMUNICATE, COMMUNICATE, COMMUNICATE.

Communication is the most important part of any business relationship. Without communication, a good partnership cannot be established between you and your assistants.

Far too often I have heard authors talk about how their assistant is not doing things they expected them to do. And when I have asked if they outlined what they wanted the assistant to do and communicated their expectations, the answer was often no or 'perhaps not clearly enough.'

As much as we might wish it was the case, assistants are not mind readers. They will not know what you want or if you want them to do things differently or change to publishing schedule, taking on other tasks or other things. If you do not tell them what you want, they will not know and that is not fair to them.

And communication, of course, goes both ways. Your assistant needs to communicate with you on what they are working on, what they need from you, deadlines approaching, etc.

Establish how you want to communicate early in the partnership. I suggest some sort of messenger service, like Slack, Discord, or Facebook Messenger, for communications that need to be addressed in real time.

Email is good for forwarding specific requests or connecting your assistant with someone reaching out to you for newsletter swaps, social media swaps, etc. It is also a good way to make sure certain things are communicated where they can be found—like days off, vacations, etc., where the assistant would need to cover for you. And vice versa—so the assistant can let you know in writing where it can be easily found when they have vacations or other things planned.

And if something is urgent or needs to be explained in more detail than you would like to go into on a messenger service or email, call them or schedule a Zoom meeting. It does not hurt to have a verbal conversation and sometimes it helps—a lot.

It might also be a good idea to schedule a meeting once a month—perhaps at the beginning of the month—to talk about anything you want done in the next month and to review the previous month.

DO NOT UNDERESTIMATE OR OVERESTIMATE HOW LONG TASKS WILL TAKE.

This is something even I struggle with, past and present. I am terrible about under-estimating how long some tasks will take or thinking I can get a lot more done in a day than I can. This is especially true for a new task they are still learning, creating graphics or other tasks that may take more time than others based on sites running slow or other problems.

What may have taken one assistant, or yourself, a shorter amount of time may take them longer and vice versa.

I have sped up immensely as I learned how to fine tune and make better use of my time, including tasks to do together as a group or how to be more efficient at certain tasks. Each assistant will be different, but as they are learning, expect tasks to take more time until they are comfortable with them and figure out how to be more efficient at it for themselves.

DEFINE YOUR EXPECTATIONS.

It is hard to live up to someone's expectations if you do not know them. This is especially true for a virtual assistant.

Whether you want them to do regular newsletters, schedule social media, or spend a certain amount of time doing certain tasks, they need to know that.

Or if you want them to join a set number of book promos in StoryOrigin or Bookfunnel, newsletter swaps, or something else, it is good to relay that to them.

If your expectations change or grow, be sure to let them know that, too.

Assistants also need feedback, especially when they are new to working for you. It takes time for an assistant to understand how you want things worded in newsletters or social media or to make graphics how you like them, etc.

Providing constructive feedback is a great way for them to learn and grow.

BE FLEXIBLE.

Understandably, there are some tasks that need to be done by a certain date. But real life happens. Whether they have an appendix go out, a death in the family, or just need to take some time off, be sure to be flexible with them. If you can pick up some tasks while they're out, great. If not, and you need a backup to assist, go that route. They may even have someone in mind to help cover them while they're out.

Be sure to discuss with them any known travel plans or events coming up at least once a year.

Be sure to communicate with them about any upcoming travel plans, medical procedures, or other events when they come up. It is understandable that if there's an emergency and you can't tell them, but if it happens a lot, it can be an inconvenience for them, especially if they need questions answered and you are gone and they did not know you were going to be gone.

IF THINGS ARE NOT WORKING OUT, DO NOT HESITATE TO END A RELATIONSHIP.

The person might be a good assistant, but might not be the best fit for you.

Whether there is a personality conflict, tasks not being completed on time, or anything else, letting them know it is not working out and you are parting ways is not fun, but it is necessary. Working with an assistant that is not working out adds more stress to that you do not need.

While it may mean taking on some tasks until you find a replacement and interviewing another person or two, it will work out for the best.

No one enjoys letting an employee go. But it is part of the process and they should understand the reasons as well.

ASSISTANTS NEED TO BE PAID.

I have seen this conversation a few times in various author groups where an author needs help, but does not want to pay for an assistant and are looking for volunteers.

I will quote a phrase used often by myself and others over the past few years.

"You get what you pay for."

If you expect an assistant to volunteer for you because they are gaining experience or exposure, rethink that.

Every assistant is worthy of being paid—even if they are new and learning the ropes. They may start out at a lower rate, then increase rates as time progress.

Justifying lack of payment because you are teaching them is wrong. You would have to educate an assistant on your wants and needs and they would be paid more for already being experienced. No single assistant is perfect or a mind reader, so keep that in mind.

The other phrase I want you to remember is "Time is money."

It comes from a video game, but the statement is real.

Time equals money. If you expect someone to spend their time so you can make money by spending your time writing, then they are worthy of being paid for their time.

OTHER QUESTIONS

There may be other questions you are asking yourself at this point in the book, I have tried to answer the other ones I thought authors might have below.

Questions in this section include:

- I write for an indie/traditional/hybrid publisher. Would an assistant be useful?
- I am not sure I need an assistant; what would you say to convince me?
- I want to hire an assistant, but I do not know where to find one. Can you help?
- Why should I take a risk on an inexperienced assistant? Is it worth the risk?

I WANT TO HIRE AN ASSISTANT, BUT I DO NOT KNOW WHERE TO FIND ONE. CAN YOU HELP?

That is a complicated question that I do not have the best answer to.

There are several Facebook groups dedicated to virtual assistants, but many of them are not just for authors. If you will work with the right person and train them to do what you need them to do for your author business, it might just be a beneficial relationship.

I would suggest looking into one of the many groups that has virtual and personal assistants for authors, looking through the 20Booksto50k Facebook group for their posts for virtual assistants or people posting ads within dedicated posts there. You could also Google for "author personal assistants" or "author virtual assistants" and check out the various websites that come up to see if they have availability.

Some assistants have a second profile with their name followed by PA (ie. Grace Snoke PA). You could reach out to them and see if they have an availability.

My last suggestion is to ask authors whom you know have an

assistant. They may know if their assistant is looking for more work or if they may know other assistants interested in helping.

Note: Some of the newsletter promotion sites also have additional services they provide to authors, including virtual assistant work. Zero Alchemy is one site I can think of off the top of my head that has this available.

I have also created a group dedicated to helping authors and virtual assistants connect on Facebook. Search for "Authors looking for P.A/V.As looking for Work" with Grace Snoke as an admin. Answer the questions to gain admittance. I will be actively recruiting assistants to join the group as well.

I WRITE FOR AN INDIE/TRADITIONAL/HYBRID PUBLISHER. WOULD AN ASSISTANT BE USEFUL?

If you have the income to justify having an assistant, the answer would most definitely be yes.

It really does not matter if you have a publisher or are independently publishing yourself. An assistant can take a lot of the work off your shoulders, leaving you more time to write. And those tasks are the same—except for handling ARC Teams, proofreading and a few other tasks.

Most indie and traditional publishers still require you to market and promote your own books and maintain your social media. Rarely do they run it for you and even if they did, you still need to play a role in being a relatable person to your audience.

Newsletters still have to be sent out, social media posts scheduled, promotions booked, and more.

If you are a traditionally published author, you know you have sales goals to meet and that you have to play a hand in marketing just as much as the publisher does. Your assistant can help with that. Just make sure they are not stepping on the toes of your publisher or that they are not supposed to do certain things because of the contract.

If you are an indie published author, while an indie publisher has their own reach, you have yours. You still need to build your own mailing list, your own social media and your own reach, which ultimately will allow you to sell more. And with the changes Amazon has made to ads, you can now also run ads on your books that have been published through your publisher—just make sure you do not shoot yourself in the foot by doing so (if, for example, they are already running ads for it, it might not be beneficial for you to run ads on Amazon as well).

Be sure to consult your contracts and verify what the publisher is doing or not doing for you before you bring on an assistant so that you know what work you can ask for help with.

I AM NOT SURE I NEED AN ASSISTANT; WHAT WOULD YOU SAY TO CONVINCE ME?

Do you want more time to write books?

Do you want to level up your author career (whether that means make more money in the long run, publish more books, collaborate with more authors, or something else)?

Do you want to get rid of tasks you do not want to do?

Do you hate [insert marketing/ads/newsletters/social media/other task here]?

Do you want more family time?

If you answered yes to one or more of these questions, then I think you need an assistant.

And I will do one better. I recently had to hire an assistant because I have acquired more work than I can feasibly do regularly and keep up with my writing—this book was behind a few months because of this and courtesy of my assistant, I could take vacation and spend some time writing to get caught up. So if that does not convince you, I am not sure what else I could say that would!

WHY SHOULD I TAKE A RISK ON AN INEXPERIENCED ASSISTANT? IS IT WORTH THE RISK?

I will be biased on this answer because I was an inexperienced assistant when I started out in 2019. I had done a bit of volunteer work for authors, but not a lot, and the work I had done for those authors wasn't in the same genres I wanted to break into. While I have extensive knowledge in several genres, I was really looking to work in the genres I would eventually publish in.

I think it can be worth the risk because you can build a relationship that lasts for years working with an inexperienced assistant. But they should have external experience which would lead into them being a good assistant.

Someone who has a project management background, or someone who is an author themselves and is looking to make extra money being an assistant are just two examples of people who could be a good match even if they do not have experience.

I, for example, was a director of communications with more than a decade as a web administrator and corporate journalist. I was used to juggling a bunch of different tasks throughout the day and week to meet the demands of the company's clients. This worked out well for me being a virtual assistant for the same reasons. I often have to switch between tasks for multiple clients (or sometimes the same clients) to meet required deadlines.

It is an excellent opportunity to have a conversation with a potential assistant to see what their experiences are to decide if it will be a risk and how much of a risk it would be.

SUGGESTED READING FOR VIRTUAL ASSISTANTS

There are several books available which I think are useful for any assistant to have read, especially if there are tasks you want them to take on. And, admittedly, some of these were books I read when I became an assistant or while working as an assistant.

Keep in mind, there are a variety of topics in the books below. Not all of them will be appropriate for your assistant to read—especially if they are an experienced assistant. Others would not be appropriate if they are not taking on these tasks.

For reference, many of these books are by authors who attend and speak at the 20Booksto50k conference in Las Vegas and have extensive experience in the topics they are writing on. While many of these target authors doing these tasks for themselves, it would help an assistant out as well. I would suggest having read the books yourself before recommending your assistant take the time to read them.

This is not a comprehensive list, nor is this an endorsement of the books, but I think you should choose books for your assistant to read—including ones you may have read as an author to help you build your career.

- 7 FIGURE FICTION: How to Use Universal Fantasy to SELL Your Books to ANYONE by T Taylor
- Ads for Authors Who Hate Math: Write Faster, Write Smarter by Chris Fox
- Amazon Ads for Indie Authors: A How-to Guide from an Industry Expert by Janet Margot
- Amazon Decoded: A Marketing Guide to the Kindle Store (Let's Get Publishing Book 4) by David Gaughran
- Amazon Keywords for Books: How to Use Keywords for Better Discovery on Amazon (The Amazon Self Publisher Book 1) by Dale L. Roberts
- BookBub Ads Expert: A Marketing Guide to Author Discovery (Let's Get Publishing Book 3) by David Gaughran
- Help! My Facebook Ads Suck: Second Edition (Help! I'm an Author 1) by Mal Cooper and Jill Cooper
- Help! My Launch Plan Sucks (Help! I'm an Author Book 2) by Mal Cooper and Jill Cooper
- Help! My Blurbs and Ad Copy Suck: Learn an Easy and Fun Process for Writing Blurbs and Ad Copy (Help! I'm an Author Book 3) by Mal Cooper and Jill Cooper
- Help! My Marketing Strategies Suck (Help! I'm an Author Book 4) by Mal Cooper and Jill Cooper
- How To Market A Book: Third Edition (Books for Writers Book 2) by Joanna Penn
- How to Write a Sizzling Synopsis: A Step-by-Step System for Enticing New Readers, Selling More

Fiction, and Making Your Books Sound Good by
Bryan Cohen
- Launch to Market: Easy Marketing For Authors
  (Write Faster, Write Smarter Book 4) by Chris Fox
- Newsletter Ninja by Tammi Labrecque
- Newsletter Ninja 2 If You Give a Reader a Cookie by
  Tammi Labrecque
- Promotional Strategies for Books: How to Market &
  Promote Your Book (The Amazon Self Publisher 2) by
  Dale L. Roberts
- Release Strategies: Plan your self-publishing schedule
  for maximum benefit by Craig Martelle
- Relaunch Your Novel: Breathe Life Into Your Backlist
  (Write Faster, Write Smarter Book 6) by Chris Fox
- Strangers To Superfans: A Marketing Guide to The
  Reader Journey (Let's Get Publishing Book 2) by
  David Gaughran
- The Writer's Guide to Amazing Book Blurbs (Fiction
  Writing Tools 6) by S.A. Soule
- The Writer's Guide to Indie Book Promotion (Fiction
  Writing Tools 7) by S.A. Soule
- Writing Killer Cover Copy (Indie Inspiration for Self-
  Publishers Book 2) by Elana M Johnson
- Writing and Marketing Systems (Indie Inspiration for
  Self-Publishers Book 3) by Elana M Johnson
- Writing and Launching a Bestseller (Indie
  Inspiration for Self-Publishers Book 4) by Elana M
  Johnson

Your assistant should also read at least your most popular
series first to make sure your work is something they want to work
with. You may choose to gift them Amazon copies of your books or
send them digital versions via email. They need to have read at

least some of your books to know what they are working with and have conversations with you about targeted marketing if that is a task they will help with. Eventually, they should read more of your books as they continue to work with you, especially as they market them or if they build a wiki or series bible for you.

CONCLUSION

This book was a labor of love dedicated to authors who have been asking over and over what an assistant can do for them.

I have attempted to cover as many tasks as possible that an assistant can do, including tasks I personally will not take on but other assistants will.

I hope this book gives you a solid grasp of what tasks you an assistant could take on for you, and a way for you to narrow down what you would like your assistant to take on before hiring one.

I welcome feedback and suggestions for the next edition on any tasks or questions I may have overlooked.

NEWSLETTER

Interested in learning about additional non-fiction books for authors or for authors interested in being an assistant?

Sign up for my newsletter.

You'll receive emails maybe twice a month (most likely less) and as a thank you for signing up, I will send you the list of questions to ask yourself and to ask an assistant as a worksheet for you to use when hiring an assistant.

https://spiderwebzdesign.net/newsletter/

AUTHOR NOTES SEPTEMBER 22, 2022

A certain author (who I am certain most of you know) by the name of Michael Anderle has insisted to me about the importance of author notes. And while he may not be wrong (the jury is still out on that), I figure he probably has a good idea about doing them for fiction novels. I figured I'd just go ahead and add them to my non-fiction as well.

Thank you for reading all the way to the end of this book and my author notes! It means a lot.

If you liked this book (or even if you didn't) leave me a review so I know how to improve future books

The idea for this book came around this time last year. I started surveying authors then about if they could get rid of certain tasks, what would they be. After talking with authors at the 20Booksto50k 2021 conference and answering many questions about what a virtual assistant does and can do for authors, I decided to go forward with this book as well as a plan to create books for those interested in becoming personal assistants.

This is not my first foray into writing non-fiction. Prior to launching my business, I wrote non-fiction for more than 12 years.

Creating an outline for a non-fiction book came to me naturally (I still can't do them for fiction).

So that's where I began—creating an outline and then writing.

But real life kept getting in the way and then I realized something. I needed an assistant. Yes, the writer of this book who talks about how an assistant can help you do more of what you want to do—write—needed an assistant to reduce her work load so she could write.

So I brought on a friend who launched her own business and as I get more work, she's getting more work so I can spend more time writing both non-fiction and fiction books.

I did not get the book written and published when I had first intended (mid-July 2022) before the Romance Writers of Australia Conference where I spoke on this topic, but as of this writing, it will be published by mid-October 2022 and will be available before the next 20BooksTo50k conference where I'll be speaking on the topic.

I next plan to work on a series of books targeted at authors and readers who are interested in becoming virtual assistants. They will be tied to courses to help interested individuals learn how to become a successful assistant. I plan to co-author with individuals who are experts in their specialization as an assistant to provide better details on topics I'm not intimately familiar with—like Amazon and Facebook ads.

All while being an assistant and working on my fiction books.

In conclusion, I need a clone.

After discussing it with my significant other, I have also decided to offer one-hour consultation sessions to help authors figure out what tasks would work best for them to hire an assistant for. Sessions will run $60 an hour, but if you use the code **FYT2022** (put it in the email to me), it will be discounted to $45. I only have a few slots each week, so if that is something you are considering, be sure to check it out https://spiderwebzdesign.net/virtual-assistant-consultation/.

I hope this book helped you find out what tasks you want to get rid of and that you find an assistant that meets your needs!

-Grace

ABOUT THE AUTHOR

Grace Snoke is an avid writer who has been writing for as long as she can remember.

Widowed in her late 30s, she is now a 40-something year old with an adult son, Richard, and two house panthers, Odin and Loki. She has a significant other who resides in Australia and she hopes to eventually end up there with him.

For many years she was a corporate journalist moonlighting as a corporate journalist for many years. She wrote for several major game sites and occasionally misses the work. Now she works as a virtual assistant, moonlighting as an author. She hopes to be a full-time writer one day.

In addition to her non-fiction projects, she is working on two urban fantasy series and a paranormal romance series in her own urban fantasy universe.

For more information about her virtual assistant and web site services, visit https://spiderwebzdesign.net.

For more information on her books, visit: https://gracesnoke.com

Connect with her on social media:

Facebook:
https://www.facebook.com/SpiderwebzDesign

Facebook:
https://www.facebook.com/AuthorGraceSnoke

Instagram:
https://www.instagram.com/kayhynn/

TikTok (no videos yet but soon...maybe?):
https://www.tiktok.com/@kayhynn

ACKNOWLEDGMENTS

Many thanks to James Osiris Baldwin for editing this book and fixing some of my errors. It's greatly appreciated.

Thanks to Craig Martelle, Martha Carr, Michael Anderle, and LMBPN Publishing. Without Craig's recommendation to Martha that I might make a good assistant and without Martha deciding to take a risk, I wouldn't be where I am today and I wouldn't have as much knowledge as I have now about being a virtual assistant.

Thanks to Kelly O'Donnell for helping me sort out the formatting for the book and doing a proofread for me.

www.ingramcontent.com/pod-product-compliance
Lightning Source LLC
Chambersburg PA
CBHW022330280326
41934CB00006B/592